# This book belongs to

_____

Write your name now
and take mastery of the contents!

"Simple and easy. It is very good to learn how to write the letters and connect them. I would definitely recommend this..."

Marina Saleeb, USC student

"It was very explicit. It drills things into your head well. It makes Arabic easy to learn. Simplifies what is generally perceived as a difficult language."

Amy Herrmann, USC student

"I like the creativity of the ways to learn the letters and the integration of the Arabic letters into the pictures. It is a unique and creative way to learn the Arabic Alphabet."

Travis, USC student

"Different. Very creative.
...It's a different and creative way to learn Arabic."

Alex, USC student

"Teaches the alphabet in a novel way, instead of just by rote. It's an easy way to learn the Arabic alphabet that isn't boring."

Otis Clarke, USC student

"I liked the visual, oral combination. By combining the visual of writing it and listening to it, I learn it better. Also, the names (Meem Mung bean sprouts) & Genie would definitely help learners remember. Definitely sticks in mind.
...I would say that it is very accessible, it is easy to learn and remember the letters. Good for learning on your own, too."

Catherine Lyons, USC student

**W**elcome to the start of an exciting adventure-- one that is going to last you well for the rest of your life. Other people might remain unknowing and unable to read, but you got this book-- _you are_ smart--whether you know it already or not. Maybe you might have been uncertain in the past--perhaps even a little scared. But now you realize how **important** it is to learn your letters **well**, so that you <u>actually</u> remember them. And that's why you're here!

Just imagine the great feelings you'll get after you've successfully finished this course. You can read the Arabic letters on road signs, and drive safely. You can read the Arabic letters on menus, and order food with confidence. And, most importantly of all, you will never again be lost in a sea of unfamiliar scribbles. After you finish this course, and have fun faithfully doing all of the playful exercises, you will achieve mastery over the letters in the Arabic alphabet. You will be able to call each one out by name. You will be able to read each letter, and say its sound. And yes, you will even be able to write the letters yourself.

## <u>You</u> will

# Actually Learn Arabic Letters!

# Actually
# Learn Arabic Letters

A Fun Course That Works--In 3 Weeks

Week 1
'Aalif through Dhaal
*with four bonus symbols*

by Real World Peace

AUTHORITY BOOKS, INC.  AUSTIN, TX

Real World Peace is dedicated to promoting pragmatic, sustainable peace in the real world through enabling communication; raising standards of living; creating basic understanding; and giving people the tools they need to run their own lives well. For more information, please go to http://www.realworldpeace.org

# Actually Learn Arabic Letters
## A Fun Course That Works--In 3 Weeks
## Week 1 'Aalif through Dhaal *with four bonus symbols*
by Real World Peace

Ⓐ
Published by Authority Books, Inc.
Premiere Edition / First Printing, 2009

Authority Books, Inc.
100 Congress Ave Suite 1100
Austin, TX
78701-4042
United States of America
http://www.authoritybooks.com

ISBN-13: 978-1-886275-02-7
(ISBN-10: 1-886275-02-5)

Go ahead and check out
**http://www.authoritybooks.com/arabic.html**
for some free stuff that will help you out.

Authority
Books

# Preface

This is the book I wish I had been given when I was learning Arabic letters. It is designed, using the latest scientific methods, to be *the* definitive course on ACTUALLY learning Arabic letters. Other courses are hard, and then their results simply don't stick. But you'll find that the catchy poems and fun, weird images of our course stick in your mind no matter what, with practically no effort whatsoever.

Most people in other courses spend a little bit of time and effort memorizing letters going in. They then have to spend a great deal of time and effort making themselves try to recall the letters when they need to, for the rest of their life. It is because there was never anything different about the memories of the letters. They were all just spikes and dots.

This poor scenario is completely backwards from the way it should be.

We have spent two years of time and specialized effort in making each letter unique and screamingly memorable. As a result, all you need to do is to invest the 10 or 20 minutes of your time needed to actually accomplish the fun exercises--and you've got the knowledge of the letter literally locked in at your fingertips, for life. Recall simply jumps out at you.

This is the right way to do things. Spend a few extra minutes up front, and have the rest of your life be easy.

This is why it simply makes so much sense to invest the time up front and actually do the exercises. The quality of your results will depend upon the quality of the attention that you put in. We've put so much effort into making this easy for you--and all you have to do is the last part. So please go ahead and put in just a little bit of time to complete the exercises, and this will ensure a high quality of learning for you that will stick with you for the rest of your life.

Will this book make you fluent in Arabic all by itself? Of course not. Language consists of letters--vocabulary words--pronunciation--grammar---sentences--reading--writing--speaking--listening, and conversation skills. Of these, this course can only teach you letters, introductory reading and writing, and some pronunciation. However, the letters are the foundation upon which everything else can be built.

When you have a solid foundation, everything else proceeds strongly from there. When you have a weak foundation, you spend all your time trying to remember the basics, and it's difficult to get further. Here we sink in a strong base. Vocabulary words and grammar would follow next.

If you are a person in service, this course will help you accomplish your mission.

If you are an executive, this easy course will give you enjoyment while broadening your mind. You can pick it up like Sudoku in spare minutes.

If you're a kid, we don't need to explain all this to you--you get what the book is about already.

Finally, if you're a college student, kindly please bear with us. The executives know that their time is very valuable--they want something laid back, simple and easy, that actually works, and that takes as little time as possible to be effective. Most of the undergraduate college students we interviewed said that the course was too easy (!). They wanted something hard--without any silly pictures or weird poems--something serious that they would have to work hard at for 12 weeks and then maybe it would work. You can certainly find other courses like that, but this isn't one of them. Here's a secret...this is in fact the senior executive's version, cleverly disguised as a book that can also be used for others, including children.

And if you find yourself having fun while you're finishing the exercises, sshhh...you'll just want to tell your friends, or anyone else who's serious about learning Arabic. You don't need to let your instructor know...

# Acknowledgments

Many thanks are due to Imam Jihad Turk, Director of Religious Affairs at the Islamic Center of Southern California, President of the Wilshire Center Interfaith Council, Vice President of the Interreligious Council of Southern California, and Arabic instructor at UCLA, for his kind words of encouragement, and for opening up his Arabic class to checking out the books. Prof. Turk's constant struggle against violence and hatred, and for peace and understanding, serve as a quiet example for all who work with him.

Many thanks are also due to PhD candidate Sarah Ouwayda of the USC Linguistics Department, for laboriously reviewing the text of all three books; for offering countless suggestions and improvements on how the course instructions could be made better; and for kindly opening up her USC Arabic class to testing out the course.

To Sara Al-Faresi, Vice President of Foreign Affairs of the National Union of Kuwaiti Students USA, thank you for believing in the project and for opening up your conference to the group.

To the Arabic students of USC and UCLA who so graciously served as test subjects, gave comments, and kindly allowed their names to be used, we are truly grateful. In alphabetical order: Alex (USC), Otis Clarke (USC), Eddie (UCLA), Amy Herrmann (USC), Catherine Lyons (USC), Kamal Moummad (UCLA), Wendy Radwan (UCLA), Marina Saleeb (USC), and Travis (USC). To the numerous other students who helped out and chose to remain anonymous we also offer a hearty thank you.

Any mistakes that may remain in the book are of course our fault, and not the responsibility of any of these busy commentators who kindly offered their time to advise on sections of early versions.

Mr. Johnny Casey and his base team deserve extra praise for work above and beyond the call of duty, and for providing support during the dark hours.

Exquisite thanks are due to cartoonist Phillip Shrock for his pencils and inks of the funny pictures, and for making the vision real.

Beautiful thanks are due to graphic designer Audrey Snodgrass, for her work on the third version of the covers. Graphic designer Lisa Yu worked tirelessly on much of the intricate writing instructions art work, and provided the gorgeous second edition of the covers. Rachel Hamm, Amber Howell, and Gayle Cantrell were all instrumental in pushing through the production. Great thanks go to Gay Alano for payroll, taxes, and outstanding strategic financial planning. Finally, to all the rest of the Real World Peace and Authority Books teams, many of whom believed in the project enough to sign up for deferred payment--the graphic design team, the writing team, editing, layout and production, the testing team, the marketing group, and the computer support team--hearty thanks is presented. We couldn't have done it without you.

# About "The Line"

## _The line of text_

**When** you're writing script letters in English, some letters go above the line, like a "_b_" or a "_d_". Some letters are half-height and sit on the line, like an "_i_" or an "_m_". And some letters go below the line, like a "_g_" or a "_p_".

If you were to draw the letters that are supposed to go above the line BELOW the line, or draw the half-height letters FULL height, or draw the letters that are supposed to go below the line ABOVE the line, it will look funny. It would be a _big_ mistake.

It's the same in Arabic.

So when we talk about letters being "above the line" or "below the line", it means just what you think it should mean. And most of the time, the place where the line is is going to be obvious. And we'll put a solid bar going across on the line to indicate where the *next letter* should start, on connected or unconnected letters. Note that the bar on the line is not actually part of the letter. It's just a placeholder for where the next letter starts. Since there's a big difference between connected and unconnected letters, this is going to be important.

# A Quick Summary for Smart People

Let's jump right in! Here are a handful of basic facts you need to know eventually about how Arabic works. Don't worry if you don't understand these fully right now. Just run your eyes over them and read these facts for now, and what they actually mean will become clear to you later on.

1. Arabic reads right-to-left on a line. Then the lines go top-to-bottom. After you get used to this, it's no problem.

2. Arabic is written in *script letters* (not BLOCK LETTERS). So they're connected.

3. There are NO Capital Letters.

4. Instead of Capital and small letters, there are four slightly different forms for each letter. These depend on whether the letter is *standing alone* by itself, is *starting* the word, is in the *middle* of the word, or is at the *end of* the word. We will cleverly call these the Stand-Alone Form, the Beginning Form, the Middle Form and the Ending Form, so that you can tell them apart easily. In most cases, many of these will be almost exactly the same inside one letter, so it's no big deal. Certainly it's no worse than, say, having to learn Capital "A" and small "a", I mean, they kind of look like each other but kind of look different. It's the same in Arabic. Usually the Stand-Alone form will be the fanciest, it is kind of like what we think of when we write Capital initials in script. It's the "official" portrait of the letter. Usually the Ending Form will look a lot like the Stand-Alone Form, except of course it has to be connected from the previous letter.
The Beginning Form usually looks like a shorter, more simple version, and the Middle Form often looks like the Beginning Form. You'll see.
Remember that the beginning is on the right, and the end of the word is on the left.

# A Quick Summary for Smart People (continued)

5. Almost all of the official Arabic letters are **consonants**.

6. There are only three "long" vowels in the official alphabet:
   "aa" (A),          "ii" (or "ee") (y),     and     "uu" (or "oo") (w).

7. There are only three "short" vowels:
   "a" ,              "i" (or "e"),           and     "u" (or "o").

8. Short vowels are written using "accents" (diacritic marks).
   Short vowels are not part of the official alphabet.
   Short vowels are typically **not written** in normal text for adults,
   because everyone knows what they are, anyway.

9. The long vowels are pronounced longer in time than the short vowels.
   That's why they're called "long". And that's why they're written in
   English with double letters. The sound is supposed to be the same, though.

10. Certain irregular forms, such as taa marbuuta, can also count as vowels
    such as "ah". This will all be covered later.

11. There is always a good-sized space **between** words. Just like in English.

12. **Inside** a single word, most letter forms are **connected** to the next letter
    following on the left. However, a few aren't. Like an English script *O*
    (Capital O), the letter finishes, there's a small space, and then the next
    letter has to start up again by itself. It's an **unconnected** letter.
    This will be important.

13. The next letter that follows a "connected letter" is in the Middle Form,
    because it's in the middle of the word. Unless it's on the end, of course.

14. The next letter that follows an "unconnected letter" has to start over and
    be in the *Starting Form*, because it doesn't have any line coming into it.
    Even if it's in the middle of the word. If on the end, use *Stand-Alone Form*.

# How This Course Is Laid Out

Here's what you need to know to get the most out of this course:

-- Each letter is covered in turn, in standard alphabetic order. This is important so you'll be able to look them up in a dictionary later on when you need to.

-- It takes 10 pages in a single section to cover a letter. After you go through the fun exercises, you will have this letter locked into your brain better than any other course we've ever seen.

-- In the following section, we are next going to cover briefly for you how to read these 10 pages and work with them.

-- It takes roughly 10-30 minutes to properly work through one section. This comes out to somewhere between 3 and 7 hours per book. It fits nicely into one week of a 4-to-6 hour-per-week course, if your school or training center has something like this...or a long one-day seminar, with breaks for lunch and dinner... or if you can realistically dedicate this much time per week to home study, you can cover one book in one week. Then it takes roughly three weeks to ACTUALLY learn the alphabet. So that's three books, if we keep the proper pace.

-- We have kept the course books just the right size so that they are easy to carry and so you rightfully get a real feeling of accomplishment after you finish each one. We understand that you're brave, but some other people get scared when they see a book 500 pages thick. This way breaks the alphabet course up into three bite-sized chunks that are easily managed.

# Stand-Alone Form

Here you're going to find a portrait of the main concept of the letter by itself, in all its glory.

## Name of the Letter

## English Representation
of the Letter.
What the Letter "Is".

## Ending Form

## Middle Form

leading to

## Beginning Form

leading to

(Remember that Arabic is written right-to-left.)

Is the letter a "Sun" or a "Moon" letter? More on this later.

Technical phonetics description.

...You can safely ignore this if you're not a phonetician.

Arabic Name of the Letter

Instant Messaging (IM) symbol, used by native Arabic speakers. You probably won't need this, unless you're texting your Arabic friends.

## How To Pronounce The Letter.
## Useful Stuff.

Different Popular Romanizations, used by English speakers to write down the letter in textbooks. There can be many of these.

Is the letter a "CONNECTING" letter or "NOT CONNECTING"?

This page will show you
a funny picture
and some sayings
that help you remember
the shape of the letter.
It is the most important
page in the section.
Spend lots of time
looking at this and
enjoying it.
Scrutinize the picture.

Then repeat the weird poem out loud.
Use a funny voice, or a very dramatic voice, like
Hamlet. The more funny, the better. Saying things
with your mouth, and hearing them with your ears,
makes you remember them better.

Sometimes the poem will have secret hidden
messages about the shape of the letter or its sounds,
to help you even more.

# This page will tell you useful things you need to know about the letter.

A discussion on "Moon" and "Sun" letters

Moon and Sun letters are important later on for Intermediate Arabic, and can be safely skipped if this is your first time through the books.

The Arabic word for "The" is "al". It's used a lot.

Some letters are easy to pronounce after the "L" in "al". These are normal, about what you'd expect. They don't change any. An example is the "q" at the beginning of the word for "moon"-- "qamar".
So "the moon" is spelled and pronounced "al qamar" Easy.

Historically, Arabic has decided that some letters are too hard to pronounce together with the "L" in "al" --they are too much of a tongue-twister. These are still *written* the same as always, but when they are *pronounced*, the "L" sound goes away--it changes into the next letter's sound. So you say that letter's sound twice. An example is the "sh" at the beginning of the word for "sun", "shams". So although "the sun" is *written* "al shams", it is *pronounced* "ash-shams". The L turns into the next letter's sound.

Not surprisingly, these two kinds of letters are called "moon letters" and "sun letters" in Arabic. When you start making full sentences and pronouncing them, this will become important.
Don't worry about it for now.

On this page you will get to play with sketching the funny picture. This is important. It helps you start to lock in the shape of the letter, and gives you something to think about it with. Try to picture it in your head. You can flip back to the previous page if it's not clear in your mind.

A playful mind is a mind that's thinking and remembering. Try to remember different parts of the drawing, and then play around with sketching it yourself in doodles.

The amount of time that you invest getting the basic shape down now will pay you back ten times over when it comes time to remember and write the letters.
Make sure you have fun and spend a few minutes sketching your ideas for the picture.
Maybe you can add something new onto the picture that you make up yourself!

This page will give step-by-step picture instructions
on how to draw each form.
(Remember, there are usually up to four
different forms for each letter, including
the Stand-Alone Form, the Beginning Form,
the Middle Form and the Ending Form.
Usually many of these will be repeats, so it's easier.)

The instructions for a form start at the right,
and proceed step-by-step to the left.

Each pen stroke
is numbered.
Follow the numbers
and their stroke-lines
with arrows
to tell how and
in which direction
to draw the letter.

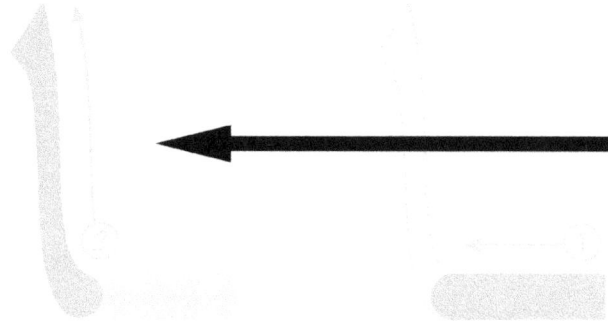

When there are multiple forms,
each form gets its own line.

Arabic letters are script letters,
and were originally drawn with a brush pen and ink.
You can see how the brush interacts with the paper.
The stroke order and direction is important.
It won't look good otherwise.

This page will complement the
How To Write It page.

| Ending Form | Middle Form | Beginning Form |

Stand-Alone Form
1. Stand-alone 'Aalif is an extremely simple letter. It's just a single straight stroke, from top to bottom. The stroke starts high and ends on the line, not below it (remember, your rocket ship is not buried in the ground).

Beginning Form
1. The Beginning Form is the same as the Stand-Alone Form — a single stroke straight down. Remember that there is nothing connected to your rocket on the left. The next letter has to start over with another

Middle Form
1. The Middle Form st
2. Without lifting pen from paper, it rounds the corner then smoothly goes straight up. Once it's to hook at the top, just lift your pen off. The down. It still does not con

Ending Form
Just the same as the Middle Form.

Some people can think better
with picture instructions.
And some people
can think better
with *word* instructions.
And there are even
some people who
enjoy having *both*.
This page gives written
instructions, for people
who prefer them.

Writing Practice

Now that you know the letter, on this page you'll get to practice actually writing each of the forms of the letter.

Writing the letter WILL help you read it later on.

Knock these out mechanically, like a football kicker practicing punting footballs through the goalposts. Bang, bang, bang. You want to get to the point where your hand writes the letter by itself, automatically. If you start getting bored, it means that you're doing it right. Finish your set anyway. 2 short minutes of boredom might save your life some day.

Do not get sloppy, though. Practice for good form. However cleanly you write in this practice could stick with you for the rest of your life. So be crisp and clean, not loose and sloppy.

The letter should fill up most of the square. Frame the letter in each square. Start over each time. Come in and go out from the square edge. Please start on the right, and write right-to-left.

We recommend using the first two lines to repeat the Stand-Alone Form; the next two for the Beginning Form; the next two for the Middle Form; and the final two lines for the Ending Form. If you have a teacher, he or she might want to do it differently, which is O.K.

In order to get the most out of this training, please say the NAME of the letter out loud each time you write it, and/or alternating with the SOUND. For instance, here you would yell "'Aalif!" or "Aah!" every time you write. Make it fun. Use a cat voice--a Martian voice--a Presley voice--a cow--something different each time. And weird. This will help lock it in for you.

Writing Practice
Now put them together.
Remember, it was four bits,
separate in your mind.

**On** this page we will give you all four forms together, and you will get to practice putting them all together on one line. (You remember Arabic goes right-to-left, right?)

The Stand-Alone form starts out by itself, of course. The Beginning Form comes next. Connect it into the Middle Form, and then follow it up with the Ending Form--the last three, all connected together on one line. You get to cross the box boundaries on this one. Remember to sound out.

━  ━  ━

...There is a controversy surrounding this exercise. For the few letters that are "unconnected" (there are only six of them), such as the 'Aalif, it really doesn't make much sense to put these together and go from a Starting Form into a Middle Form. Because: Any letter following an **unconnected** letter has to **start over** again with a Starting Form or a Stand-Alone Form, *even if it's in the middle of a word.* Because the previous letter is **unconnected**, of course.

Perhaps the right way to exercise would be to put a connected letter, such as "baa'", in between each of these. So then, instead of "A A A", you would write "A b A b A".

However, because this is a basic primer, we feel this would be more confusing for the beginning student. So, instead, we are putting an "underscore" on the line between the Starting and Middle forms, and the Middle and Ending forms. Then you are actually writing "A _ A _ A". This is cheating a little, but not very much. As long as you realize that the underscore following the letter is *not part of the letter,* it's just there to let you know that there should be something else coming afterwards, this should work out fine.

Know The Difference!

Arabic letters are easy to tell apart when you know the distinctions, what to look for.  This useful page will clear up any doubts that you might have left in your mind--by showing you how the letter being shown in this section is completely different from other letters.  After you read this page, you're sure to be able to tell the letter apart from everything else!

You might want to come back and re-read this page for each section  after you finish the whole course--you'll be able to understand it better.  In the meantime, don't worry too much about letters that we haven't covered yet.

N**ow** that you're an expert on that letter, here will be a chance to prove it. Look in these Arabic words, and try to locate the letter that you just learned. It will jump right out at you!

This is the first known Arabic lesson book that actually gives you FOUR translations for each word, to make things absolutely clear. There is the native Arabic writing. This is followed by putting the exact same Arabic letters into English, in exactly the same right-to-left order that you see them there. After this, the same word is given left-to-right, but this time any thing that's missing is filled back in. Finally you get the English meaning.

Arabic likes to cut corners. Sometimes you'll notice that some of the letters in the third word, especially the short vowels, aren't actually written there in the Arabic. This is the same as in English saying that Mr. is actually "mister", or can't is "cannot". It's no problem after you get used to it. It happens *all the time* in Arabic.

# Actually
# Learn Arabic Letters

A Fun Course That Works--In 3 Weeks

Week 1
'Aalif through Dhaal
with *four bonus symbols*

by Real World Peace

AUTHORITY BOOKS, INC.  AUSTIN, TX

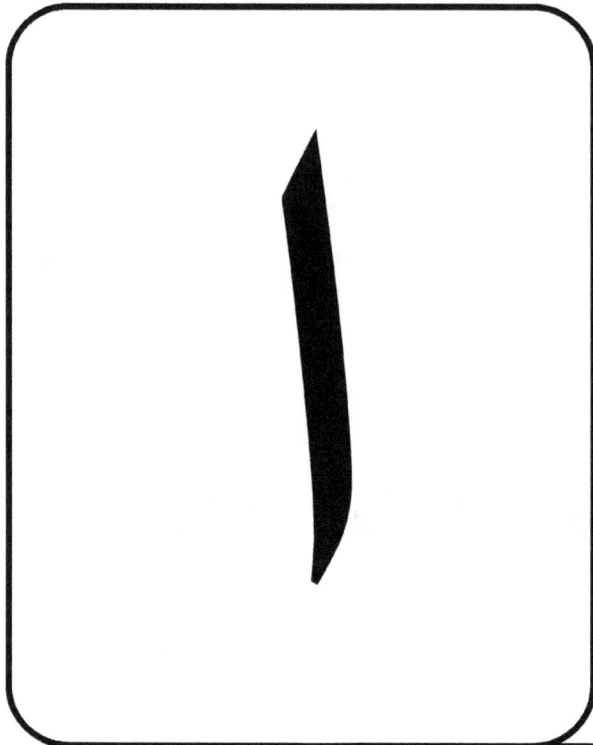

# 'Aalif

ا

aa

ل  ـل  ـا

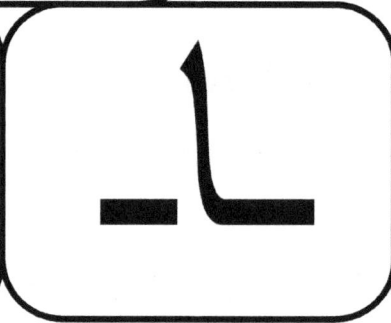

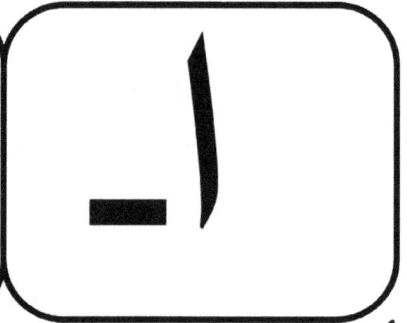

*"long low back vowel"*

أَلِف

The sound of 'aalif is the familiar "Aah" as in "father". It has a slightly longer duration than the short "a" found in "about". For this reason it is called a "long A", and it's often written "aa" to emphasize this. Sometimes this sound can move to the front of the mouth, in which case it sounds like a familiar "aa" as in "man". And after a so-called "dark letter" in the *back* of the mouth, the "aah" of "father" is actually pronounced closer to the "Oah" of "foam". But it still counts as a Long A. 'Aalif is one of only three vowel letters found in the regular Arabic alphabet.

a          *'Aalif DOES NOT connect on the left.*          aa, a, ā, A, ah, eh

# 'aalif
## is A Lift-Off

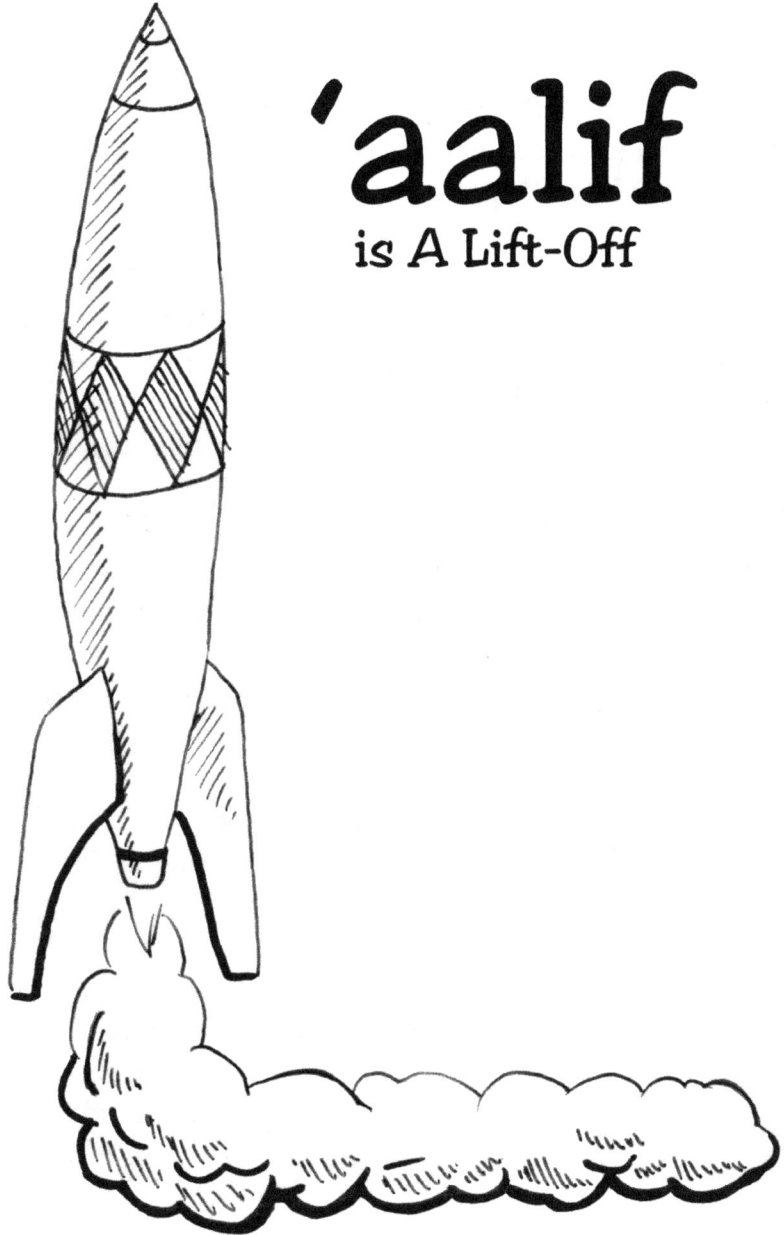

AAAaah...

Aah, aah, 'aalif, a lift-off!
Aah-some!

# Helpful Hints

Tha word "'aalif" is similar to "alpha", the old Greek name for "A". Alpha-beta is where we get our name "alphabet" from, of course. Also see the Hebrew letter "Alef".

"Ah" is one of the simplest sounds, like a sigh, that you can make. It's a sound you can make when your mouth is comletely relaxed. It's one of the first sounds that a baby makes. This is why in almost all the languages of the world the word "mama" is always the same, and the word "dada" or "pappa" is always similar, too.

The letter 'aalif is therefore one of the simplest letters, it is simply a single vertical stroke. The stand-alone or beginning version just goes straight down. The middle or ending version simply finishes by going straight up. Neither version is connected on the left-hand side with the following letter, which makes it very different from the letter Laam (L). [Laam looks like a backwards L and is connected.]

The sound "A" is the first letter of almost all alphabets in the world, including Greek, Cyrillic, Hebrew, Armenian, Oevanagari (Sanscrit), and even Japanese Hiragana and Katakana. How about that!

There are only three official vowel letters in the Arabic alphabet--
> 'Aalif (aa) [pronounced "aah"],
> Wow (w/uu) [pronounced "oo"], and
> Yaa' (y/ii) [pronounced "ee"].

These are the "long" vowels. All of the other official letters are consonants.

There are, however, also three <u>short</u> vowels. Each short vowel is supposed to be a short version of a corresponding long vowel. That is, the short vowels are brief, while the long vowels take twice as long to pronounce. The short vowels are not shown by letters in the alphabet. Instead, they are shown by little marks, similar to accent marks. We'll be covering these in the bonus section at the end of this book.

# Now You Sketch It--Doodles!

# How To Write It

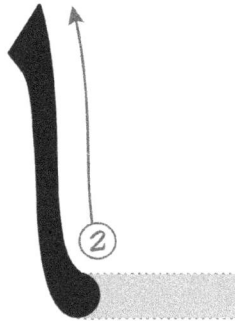

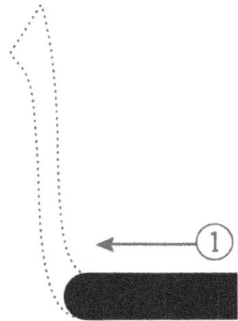

# Writing Suggestions

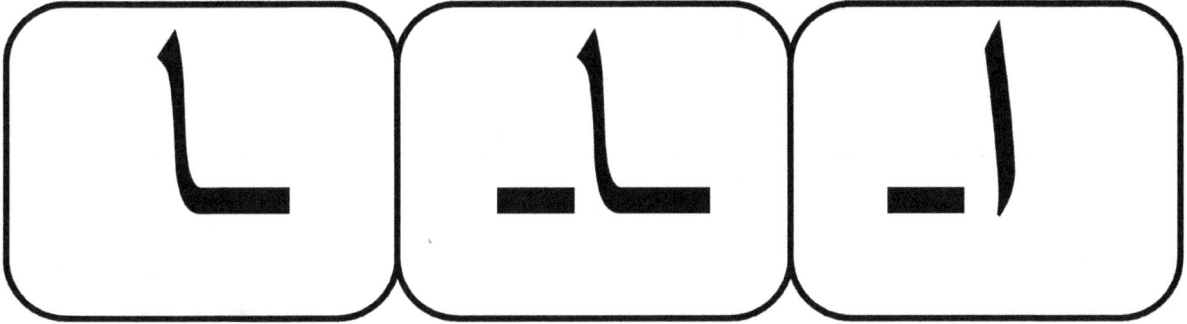

ا ـل ـل ـا

## Stand-Alone Form

1. Stand-alone 'Aalif is an extremely simple letter. It's just a single straight stroke, from top to bottom. The stroke starts high, and ends on the line, not below it--remember, your rocket-ship is not buried in the ground!

## Beginning Form

1. The Beginning Form is just the same as the Stand-Alone Form---a single stroke straight down. Remember that there is nothing connected to your rocket on the left. The next letter has to start over with another Beginning Form.    ...We don't know what your next letter is going to be. So we drew a bar on the line, after a disconnected space, to show you where the next letter goes.    The following bar is not part of the 'Aalif letter, it's just there to help you see the space after the letter and how it's unconnected.

## Middle Form

1. The Middle Form starts coming in from the right.
2. Without lifting pen from paper, it rounds off the corner, then smoothly goes straight up. There is no hook at the top, just lift your pen off. The middle form goes up instead of coming down. It still does not connect on the left.

## Ending Form

1. Just the same as the Middle Form.

# Writing Practice

Say the name of the letter, and make its sound,
each time you write the letter.

# Writing Practice

Now put them together.
Remember to keep each letter
separate in your mind.

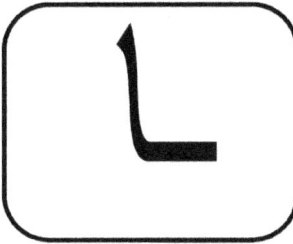

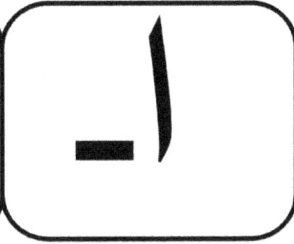

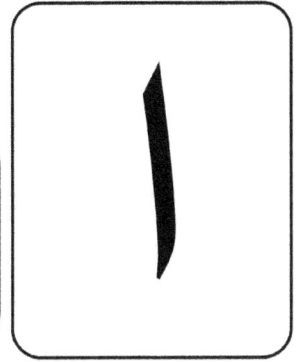

| ل | ـلـ | ـا | ا |
|---|---|---|---|
|  |  |  |  |
|  |  |  |  |
|  |  |  |  |
|  |  |  |  |

# Know The Difference!

Ending Lam goes off to the left in a backwards-L fishhook. It's square coming in from the right, not rounded at the base.

ﻝ

Beginning L has the classic backwards-L shape. It usually has a bulge at the top, and continues on to the left, joined.

ﻟ

Middle L is joined on the left side, not open. It also is square, not rounded at the base.

ﻠ

Taa' and Zaa' have a tiny minaret bump at the top of their Tall Tall Tower, and are always just to the left of their hill.

ﻂ

Final Kaaf is part of the ski-boot, which stretches off to the left side of the vertical stroke and is not open.

ﻚ

Middle LA has stuff to the left.

ﻼ

# Reading Practice

ابا

A b a

abbaa

Daddy
(Egyptian)

ال...

... l a

al...

the ...

ان

n a

an

that

انا

A n a

anaa

I, me

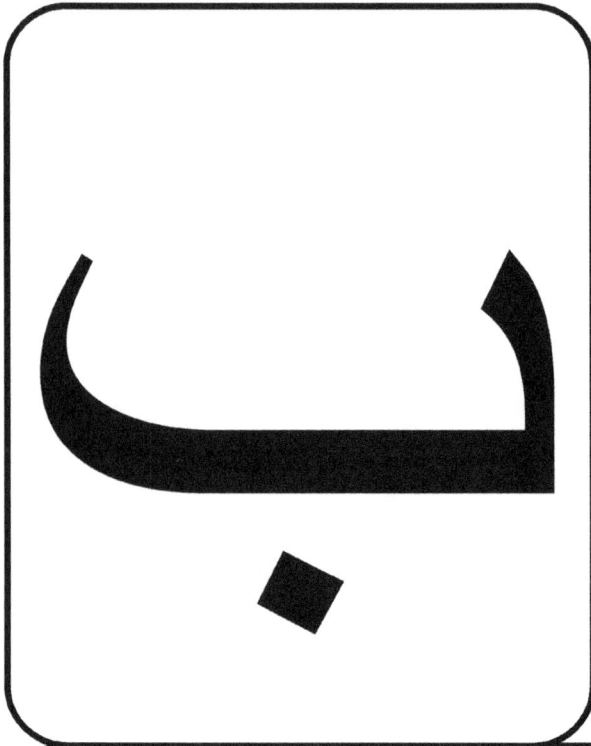

baa'

b

ب ﺑ ﺒ ﺐ

باء

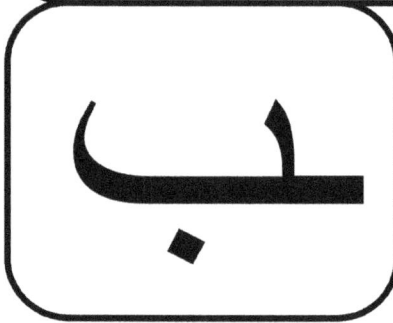

"voiced labial stop"

Baa' sounds like the familiar "B".

b          *Baa' CONNECTS on the left.*          b

# baa'

is a banana

Bahama Baa-Baa
balances a
big banana-boat
on a single
ball-bearing
BB

"baa' baa' baa',
baa ball-bearing..."

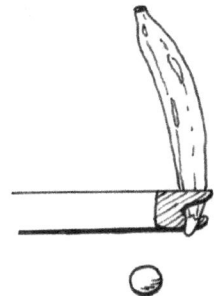

# Helpful Hints

Baa' looks like a Boat, in fact it's a Big Boat shaped like a Banana. The stem comes at the Beginning, and the fancy curve comes at the end. The middle is flat, on the line. So the dot comes below the line. In English script, we dot our "i"'s and our "j"'s above the line, but we don't have any letters that dot below the line. Try dotting on the Bottom side, Below, with the Baa'. Why not. It makes just as much sense, and it lets you get more variety in.

It's too much work to draw the entire Banana-Boat shape for the Beginning and Middle forms, so we just draw the stem to remind you and make you think about it. That's the tiny picture in the lower right.

In general, the Ending forms and the Stand-Alone forms are going to be more fancy than the Beginning and Middle forms, because there's more room to play with. The Beginning form is going to have less detail and just remind you of the official Stand-Alone form. You'll see.

Remember that the single dot for the letter "B" is "BEE-low" the line. B is low is BELOW.

# Now You Sketch It--Doodles!

# How To Write It

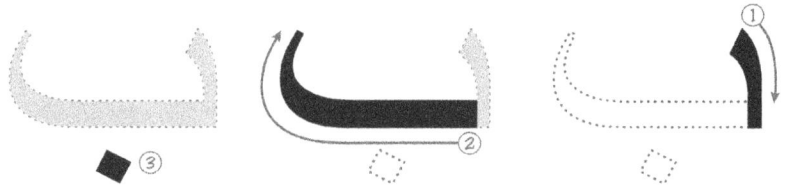

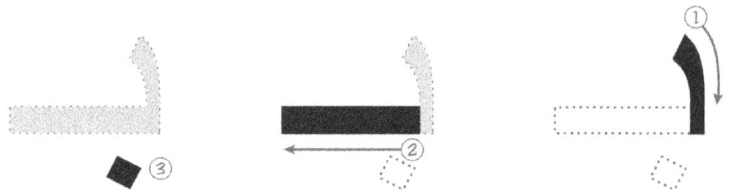

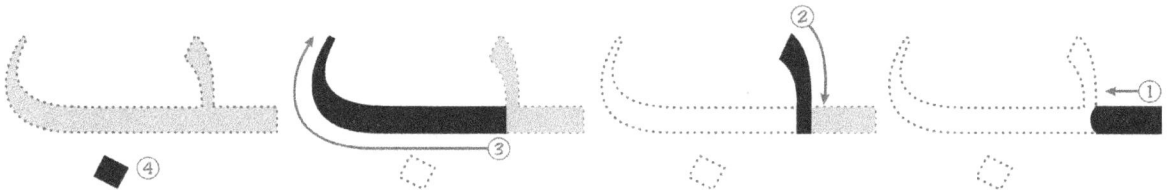

# Writing Suggestions

ب ـبـ ـب

## Stand-Alone Form

1. Start drawing your banana-boat on the right. Draw the stem first. Start slightly above the line, and come down onto the line.
2. Then draw the rest of the boat. Make it shaped like a canoe-- long, with a round part at the end.
3. Now draw your ball-bearing BB on the Bottom of the Boat. Draw this just like you dot an "i" or a "j"--no need to get fancy, but we have to see it. Dot it in the middle of the boat, so it's balanced on both sides.

## Beginning Form

1. The Beginning Form doesn't need the whole banana-boat, just the banana stem. Start halfway above the line, and come down straight onto the line.
2. Make a hard corner and continue on the line, on to the next letter.
3. Come back and dot the baa' after you're done writing the word. The dot goes almost under the banana stem, slightly following it.

## Middle Form

1. The Middle Form is similar to the Beginning Form. You're coming in from the right, from the previous letter.
2. Pick your pen up, and start halfway up to make the banana stem come straight down.
3. Make a hard corner. Continue on to the left, on to the next letter.
4. Come back later to add the dot. It goes under the banana stem, slightly following it.

## Ending Form

1. The Ending Form is similar to the Stand-Alone Form. Come in on the right, from the previous letter.
2. Lift the pen from the paper, and start halfway up, coming down to draw the banana stem.
3. Continue on the line to draw a canoe-shaped banana-boat. Make it flat, then rounded halfway up at the end. It's more than twice as long as it is tall.
4. Come back and put the BB ball-bearing dot in the middle.

# Writing Practice

Say the name of the letter, and make its sound,
each time you write the letter.

# Writing Practice

Now put them together.
Remember to keep each letter
separate in your mind.

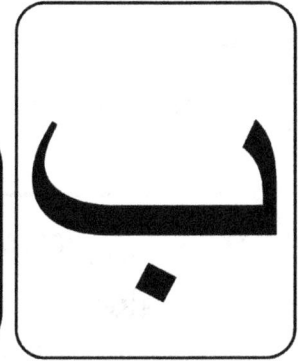

| بـب | ـبـب | بـب | بـ |
|---|---|---|---|
|  |  |  |  |
|  |  |  |  |
|  |  |  |  |
|  |  |  |  |

# Know The Difference!

Noon has one dot on TOP.
(Baa's dot is always on the "BAATTOM").

نـ ـنـ ـن

Yaa' has TWO dots on the bottom
to make the roller skate for the
Yippee yelling snake.

يـ ـيـ ـي

Taa' and thaa' have two and three dots
on TAAP. Not one dot on the BAATTOM.

ثـ ـثـ ـث
تـ ـتـ ـت

Jeem has the jackrabbit ear, it's a very
different shape from the simple banana
balanced on top of a ball-bearing BB.

جـ

Stand-alone Noon has a deeper belly,
and the single dot is above,
not Balanced Below.

ن ا

Kasrah is a mark that can come below
anything. It is a slanting slash, not a dot.

ِ

# Reading Practice

اب

b a

ab

father

ب

b

bi

by, with, at,
in, through, of

بابا

A b A b

baabaa

pope;  Papa

باب

b A b

baab

door

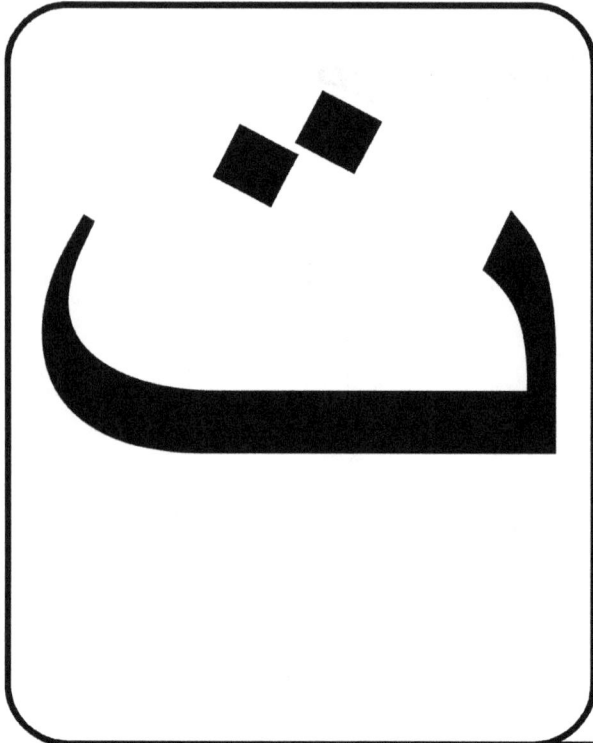

taa'

ت

t

ث ت ثـ تـ

تاء

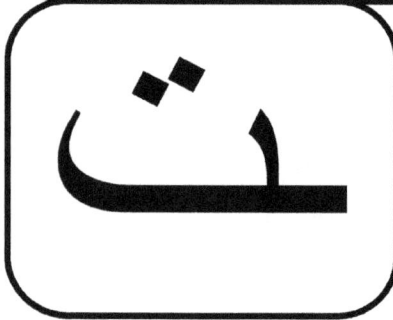

"voiceless dental fricative"

taa' always sounds like the familiar "t".
It is a light sound.

t          Taa CONNECTS on the left.          t

# taa'
## is two tots

Two tiny twin tots
(two tiny twin dots)

tasting tea
on *top*
of a Toboggin

# Helpful Hints

taa' is exactly the same shape as baa', except it has two dots on top, not one below.

The letter taa' is usually spelled in English with a small letter "t". This distinguishes it from the strong dark Taa', spelled "T", a different letter that we'll look at in the second book.

Make sure the tip of your tongue is touching your teeth in front. taa' comes from the **front** of the mouth. It's a light sound.

...There is an alternative, irregular form of the letter taa' that is used at the end of words, but only in the irregular case that the taa' is not pronounced. (It's used as a feminine marker, kind of like the "ie" in "Chrissie", "Jackie", or "Stephanie".) This is called "taa' marbuuta", or "the 't' that looks like a silent 'h'". It will be covered much later, at the end of the third book. We have to mention it here, because it falls under "taa'" in the alphabet, even though it looks different and is irregular. You don't have to worry about this one now.

# Now You Sketch It--Doodles!

# How To Write It

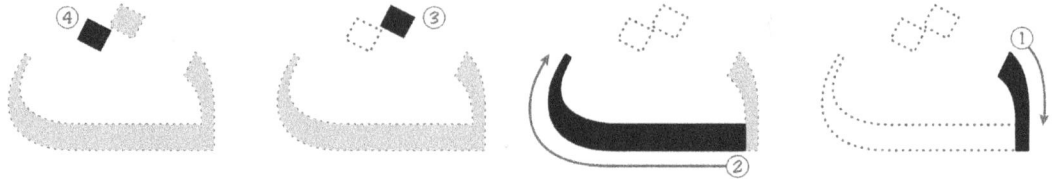

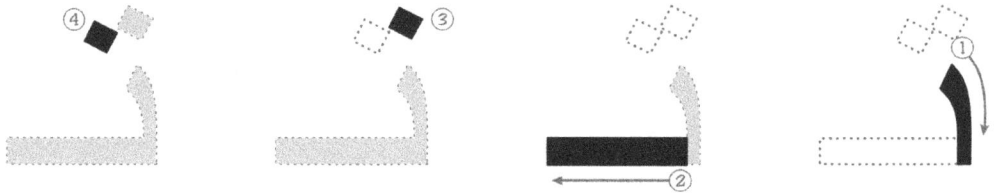

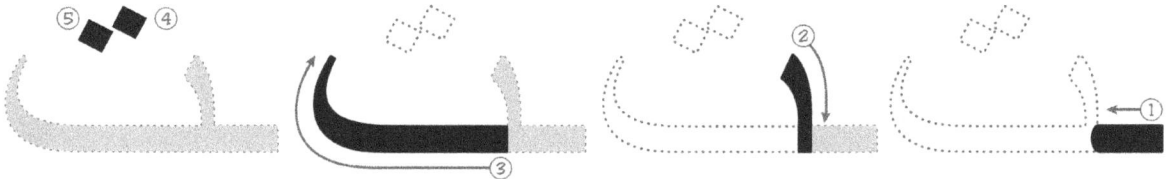

# Writing Suggestions

ﺖ  ﺘ  ﺗ

## Stand-Alone Form

1. Start halfway up and go straight down to draw the front part of the toboggin.
2. Making a hard corner, draw the long body of the toboggin on the line. Put a curve at the end. The curve is as high as the front part.
3, 4. Dot the taa' with two tiny twin dots on top. Put them in the middle, slightly above the front part and the back curve. They can be right next to each other, or slightly on a diagonal going down.

## Beginning Form

1. Start halfway up and go straight down, to draw the front part of the toboggin.
2. Make a hard corner, and continue on the line straight on to the next letter.
3, 4. Come back later and dot the taa' with two dots above the vertical part. It's like crossing a "t" later. The first dot comes right above the point, and the second dot follows afterwards.

## Middle Form

1. The Middle Form is similar to the Beginning Form. You're coming in straight, from the previous letter.
2. Pick up your pen and start halfway up. Come straight down to form the front of the toboggin.
3. Make a hard corner. Continue straight on the line to the next letter.
4, 5. Come back later and dot the taa' with two tiny twin dots above the vertical stroke.

## Ending Form

1. The Ending Form is similar to the Stand-Alone Form. You're coming in from the previous letter.
2. Lift your pen, and start halfway up. Come straight down to form the front of the toboggin.
3. Make a hard corner. Draw the toboggin long and to the left, with a curve at the end. It's more than twice as long as it is tall.
4. Dot the taa' with two tiny twin dots that go above the middle of the long toboggin. Make them float up above the front and the back curve, not sit between them.

# Writing Practice

Say the name of the letter, and make its sound,
each time you write the letter.

# Writing Practice

Now put them together.
Remember to keep each letter
separate in your mind.

ت

ـت

تـ

ـتـ

# Know The Difference!

| | |
|---|---|
| Qaaf has two dots, but they're over a loop. | ق ـق |
| Taa' Marbuuta looks like a feminine horsey or a hummingbird egg wearing a crown. It has a loop and is pronounced "Aah". | ة ـة |
| Thaa' has THREE dots. | ث ـث |
| Noon has only ONE dot. | ن ـن |
| Yaa' has two dots but they're on the bottom. Yippee! | ي ـي |
| Baa' has only one dot on the BAATTOM. | ب ـب |

# Reading Practice

بات

t A b

baata

he slept

تاج

j A t

taaj

crown

تحت

t H t

taHta

under, down,
below

بنت

t n b

bint

girl, daughter

# thaa'

**th**

ثاء

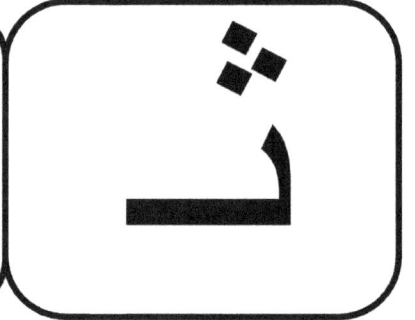

*"voiceless interdental or dental fricative"*

Thaa' is supposed to sound like the familiar soft "th" as in "thin". However, the Egyptian dialect, and some others, pronounces this closer to "t". And some dialects keep the tongue inside the mouth behind the teeth, which makes it sound like a lisped "s". Anyway, stick with "th" and you won't go wrong.

s/t/th     *Thaa' CONNECTS on the left.*     th/<u>t</u>

# thaa'

is three thistles

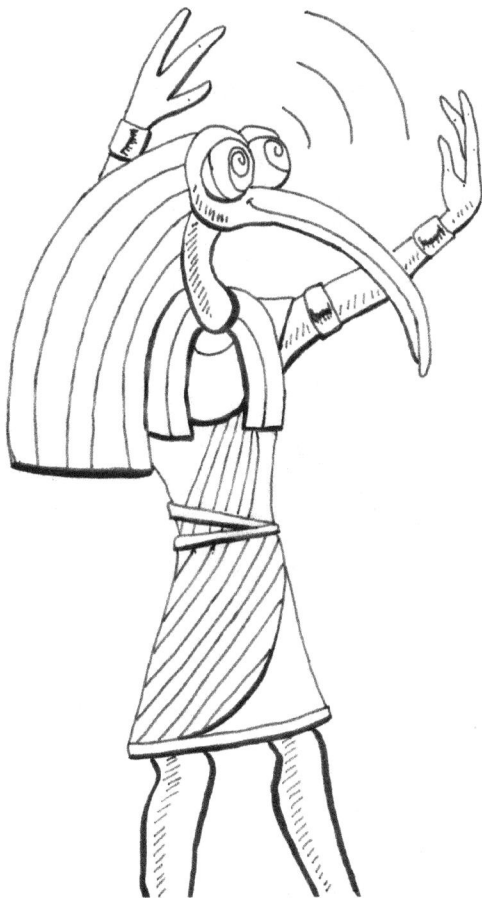

Thoth thaws
three thin
Thaa'lian
thought-
thistles.

# Helpful Hints

Unfortunately the letters "th" in English represent two different sounds, the soft "th" as in "three", and the buzzed "th" as in "this". This is also called the difference between "unvoiced" and "voiced", because you're using your voice, your vocal chords, to help make the second sound.

Thaa' is always the soft (unvoiced) "th". Because there is a big difference in Arabic between these two sounds, we will later be writing down the buzzed "th" in English as "dh", so we can tell them apart. This gets its own letter, dhaal, which you'll see later on in this book. Just remember "Three thistles for thaa'," and you'll be fine.

Thaa' uses exactly the same shape as baa' or taa', except it has **three** dots above the line.

# Now You Sketch It--Doodles!

# How To Write It

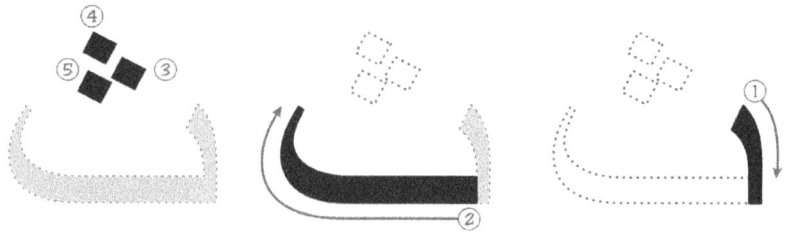

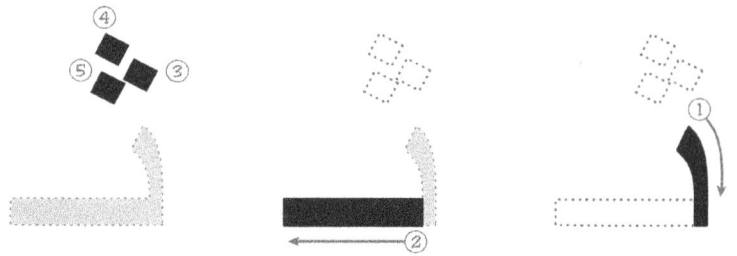

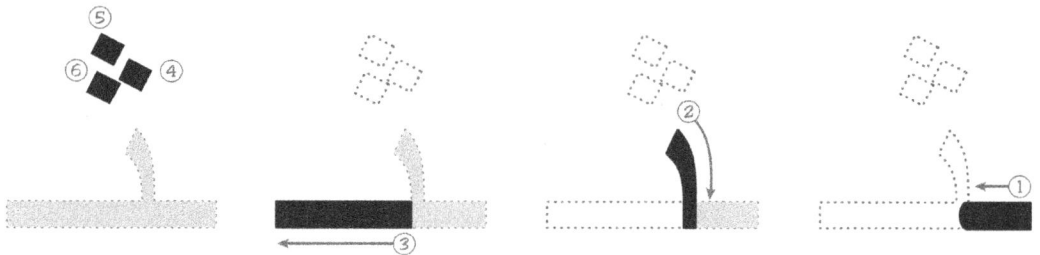

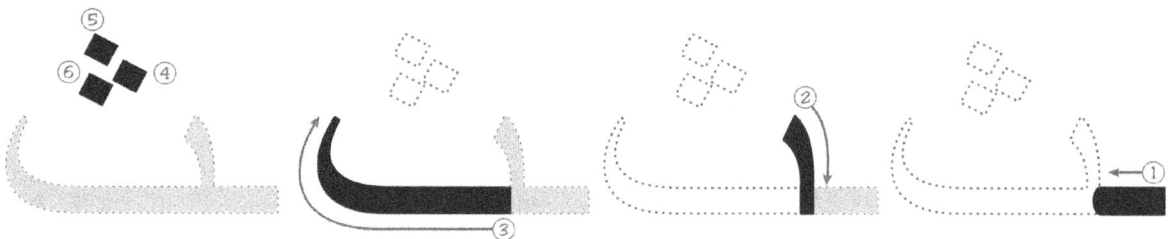

# Writing Suggestions

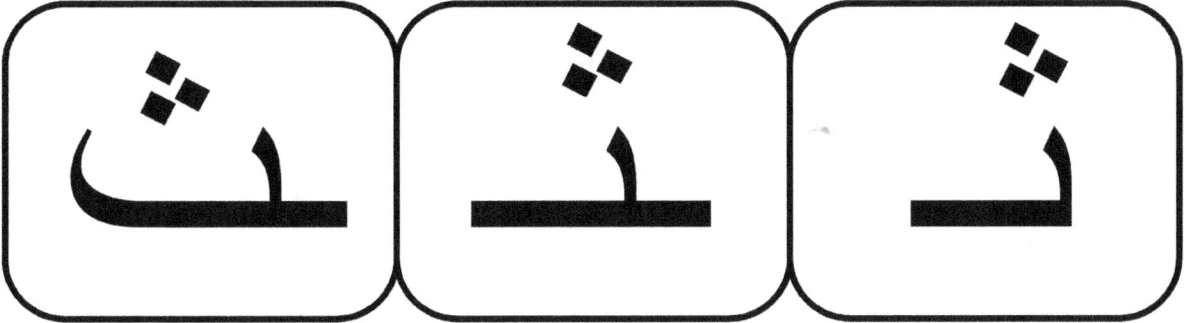

ﺚ ﺜ ﺛ

## Stand-Alone Form

1. Thaa' is quite similar to taa', except it has **three** dots on top, arranged in a small triangle or a caret. Start midway up, and draw the front of the thistle thawing-dish by coming straight down.
2. Draw the rest of the thistle thawing-dish by making a hard corner, then continuing on flat, ending with a gentle curve. The curve ends up being as high as the front part.
3. Draw the right-most thistle dot first.
4. Then draw the middle thistle dot on top.
5. Finally draw the third thistle dot on the left. These are always separate in newspaper, book, and computer printing. However, in handwriting, people will often connect these in an upside-down "v"(^).

## Beginning Form

1. Start midway up. Come straight down with a vertical stroke, to form the front of the thawing-dish.
2. Make a hard corner. Continue on the line, straight onwards to the next letter.
3, 4, 5. Come back later and put the dots over the vertical stroke. Start first with the right one, then with the middle top one, then with the left. Please make sure to get the order correct. The first dot starts directly above the vertical stroke. Then the others continue slightly to the left.

## Middle Form

1. The Middle Form is similar to the Beginning Form. You are coming in straight on the line from the previous letter.
2. Pick your pen up, and position it midway up. Then come straight down with a vertical stroke that forms the front of the three-thistle thawing-dish.
3. Make a hard corner, and continue on straight, on to the next letter.
4,5,6. Come back later to dot the thaa' with three dots. The first one is over the point, and the others follow.

## Ending Form

This is similar to the Stand-Alone Form. The three dots are drawn in the middle of the thawing-dish, not over the front part.

# Writing Practice

Say the name of the letter, and make its sound,
each time you write the letter.

# Writing Practice

Now put them together.
Remember to keep each letter
separate in your mind.

| ثـ | ثـ | ـثـ | ـث |
|---|---|---|---|
| | | | |
| | | | |
| | | | |
| | | | |

# Know The Difference!

| | |
|---|---|
| Sheen has three dots, but they are over the wavy eyeglasses. | شَـ |
| Taa' only has TWO dots on TAAP. | تـ |
| Sheen stand-alone or at the end also has the eyeglasses handle. | شـ ش |
| Qaaf only has two dots, and a loop. | قـ |
| A fat-Ha over a letter such as Daal is a single downwards slash. | دَ |
| Sheen at the beginning has three peaks in a wave, not just one peak. | شـ |

# Reading Practice

اثاث

th A th a
athaath
furniture

بث

th b
bathth
to broadcast

ثابت

t b A th
thaabit
firm, definite

ثالث

th l A th
thaalith
third

# jeem

ج

ج

ج ج ج

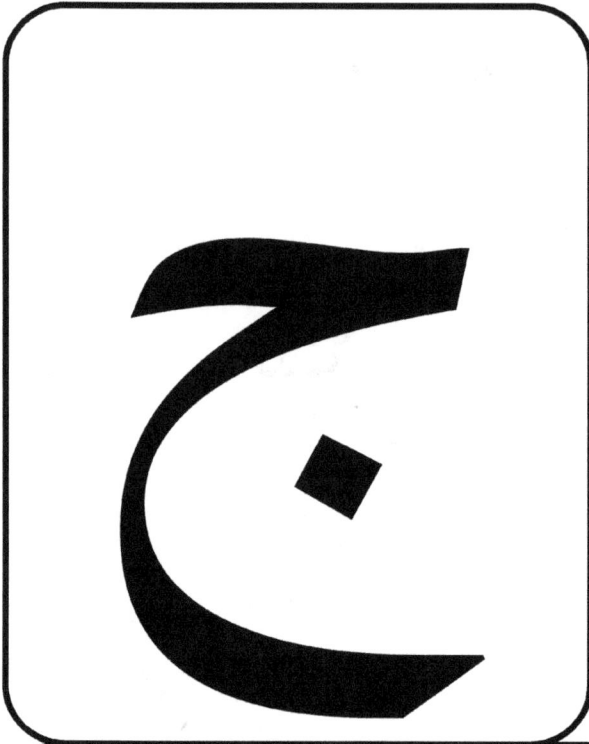

*"voiced palato-alveolar fricative"*

جيم

☪

Jeem is typically pronounced like the "zh" in the middle of "measure", or the second g in "garage". It's about the same as the French J found in "Je suis". However, Classical Arabic and the Gulf states in the east, including Iraq and the Kingdom of Saudi Arabia, pronounce this like the j in "jeep". And in the west, Egyptian Arabic hardens it into a "g" (geem), and pronounces it like the first "g" in "garage". Anyway, stick with "zh" and you won't go wrong.

j / g          *Jeem CONNECTS on the left.*          j / g / zh / ǧ

42

# jeem

is the Jolly Jackrabbit garage measure

Gee!  Jim and Gene's
one-gem Jolly Jackrabbit
garage
treasure-measure!

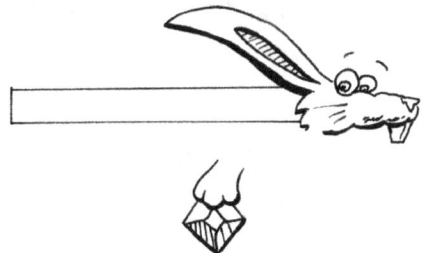

# Helpful Hints

Jeem is a big swirly letter that hangs down below the line in the stand-alone form. It is our first letter that looks pretty different between the stand-alone and ending forms, and the beginning and middle forms. That's because we don't have time to get fancy when we're writing on the line at the beginning or in the middle. You just get one swirl for the rabbit's ear, to kind of remind you of how the big stand-alone version looks, and then it keeps going on the line from there. Very business-like.

The ending form and the stand-alone form of jeem hang down beow the line significantly, like our g or j does. Please make sure to have these placed vertically properly. You don't want the ending or stand-alone jeem floating too high up in the air.

The swirl in the jack-rabbit's ear comes down sideways on a diagonal, at around forty degrees or so, on the beginning and middle forms. It's very different from the short vertical spike we see on the baa', taa', and thaa'.

Old-time watches used to use gems as the center point, the bearing, of their gears. Maybe that's why the Jolly Jackrabbit Garage Measure uses a single gem for its center-point bearing as well. Make sure the gem appears in the center, and not out close to an edge.

# Now You Sketch It--Doodles!

# How To Write It

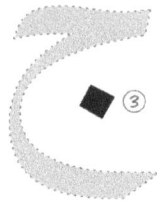

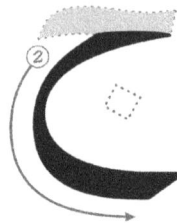

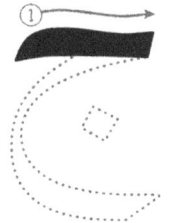

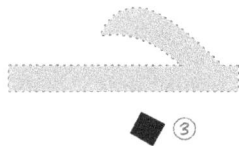

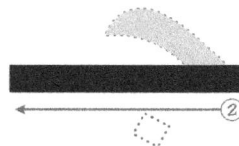

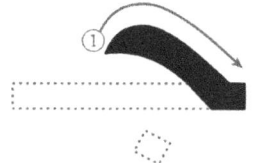

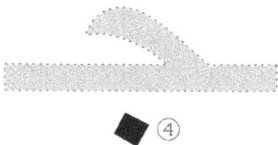

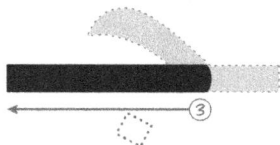

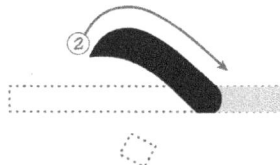

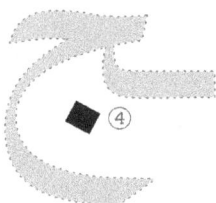

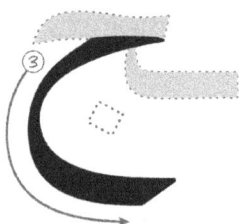

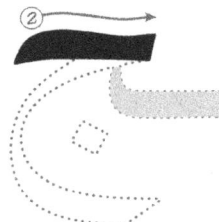

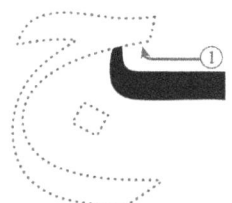

# Writing Suggestions

ﺟﺞ  ﺠﺟ  ﺟ

## Stand-Alone Form
1. Start on the left side, just slightly above the line. Draw a swirly stroke that looks like a flat jack-rabbit's ear from left to right.
2. Without lifting your pen from the paper, reverse directions and draw a sweeping curve around the top, left, and bottom of a circle. This will hang down well below the line. It defines the body of the tape-measure. The tape measure should look roughly square, with the ear being a slide-control on top. Don't make the tape measure too tall nor too fat.
3. Put the one gem as a dot in the center. It defines the axle of the tape measure.

## Beginning Form
1. Start on the left side, midway above the line. Draw a swirly diagonal stroke that looks like a jack-rabbit's ear from upper left diagonally down to the line.
2. Without lifting your pen from the paper, back up and continue straight on the line to the left, on to the next letter.
3. Come back later and put the one-gem dot underneath the jeem. The rabbit holds it on the bottom.

## Middle Form
1. You're coming in from the previous letter from the right.
2. Pick up your pen. Put it down midway up, to the left. Then come back diagonally to the right in a swirly stroke that meets the previous one. Sometimes this will actually end above the line, not meeting.
3. Without picking your pen up, reverse directions and continue on the line to the next letter. If you're actually starting slightly above the line, swirl down right to left to meet the line and continue on.
4. Come back later to put the one-gem dot under the middle of the jack-rabbit ear.

## Ending Form
1. You come in from the previous letter on the right. End with a little round hook that goes up.
2. Pick your pen up and position it to the left. Draw a swirling stroke that touches the top of the hook.
3. Without picking up your pen, reverse direction and draw a round semi-circle going below the line.
4. Finally, put the one-gem dot in the middle of the tape measure to complete the figure.

47

# Writing Practice

Say the name of the letter, and make its sound,
each time you write the letter.

# Writing Practice

Now put them together.
Remember to keep each letter
separate in your mind.

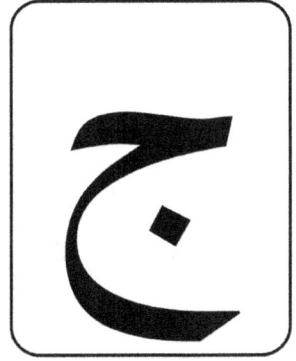

| ـجـ | ـجـ | جـ | ـج |
|---|---|---|---|
| | | | |
| | | | |
| | | | |
| | | | |

49

# Know The Difference!

Baa' has one dot on the Baattom, but it doesn't have Jolly Jackrabbit ears, just a single simple Baanana.

بـ

Haa' is a Hot empty open mouth. It has no measuring gem in the middle.

حـ

Khaa' has the point on Khan's Khap khovering the top.

خـ

Khaa' in the middle still has the point on top, not the single gem on the bottom.

ـخـ

Stand-alone Baa' has the big Banana-boat basin on the single ball-bearing BB. It forms a canoe or a dish, and is concave.

ب

Yaa' has two dots on the bottom, and no jolly jackrabbit ears for the garage measure.

ي

# Reading Practice

ثلج

j L th
thalj
ice, snow

جار

r A j
jaar
neighbor

دجاج

j A j d
dajaaj
chicken

جاء

' A j
jaa'a
to come; bring;
to be said

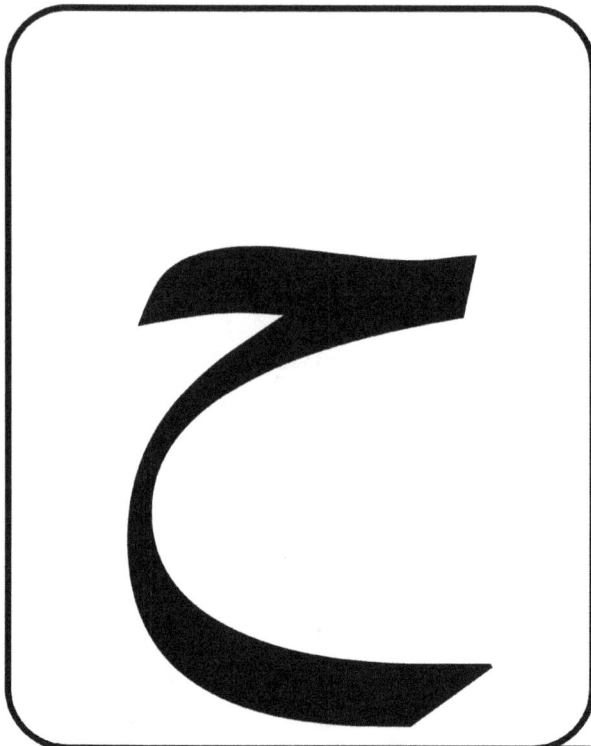

# Haa'

**H**

"voiceless pharyngeal fricative"

حَاء

Haa' is pronounced like an "H" that is scraping the back of your mouth. To say this, pretend that you just ate the hottest hot pepper imaginable. It burned your tongue, so all you can do is pant. So hot! Your mouth is on fire! This is also close to the noise you make when you are quietly trying to blow out a single candle with your mouth open, or when you are huffing on your glasses before cleaning them. It comes from the back of your mouth.

7                 *Haa' CONNECTS on the left.*                 H/ḥ/ḥ

# Haa'

## is Hot Pepper Harry

Hot Hot Harry's
empty-mouthed
Texas Hot Pepper Hero Hat.
Hot! Hot! Hot!

*HHHave a HHHot Pepper...*

# Helpful Hints

Haa' is exactly the same shape as Jeem, except it has no dot. Its shape reminds you of a hot, empty, open mouth.

Haa' is completely unvoiced. You do not hum or say ahh or anything while making this sound.

Haa', with a capital "H", is different from haa', with a small "h". We'll cover haa' later on in the third book.

How are they different, you might ask? Basically, small "h" haa' is a normal, light "h" that comes from the front of the mouth. On the other hand, our Hot capital "H" comes from the back of the mouth, as if you were trying to fog a window. It's called a "dark" H.

Haa' is our first "dark" letter. So let's take just a minute to look at this.

All "dark" letter sounds come from the back of the throat. In Arabic, these are pronounced as if there were a big bubble, an open space of air, sitting on the back of your tongue between your tongue and your throat. It's almost like you swallowed a ping-pong ball and it got stuck halfway down at the back of your mouth.

Because the dark consonants are pronounced from the back of the mouth, with the throat open, they color and change the vowel sounds around them. Any vowel sound that follows a dark letter will change. In particular, what we call a "short a" sound, found in 'Aalif as in "father", will fall back down the throat and turn into what _we_ call a "short o" sound, as in "hot / bottle". But in Arabic, these are both considered to be the _same_ sound--a long 'Aalif. So the "aah" following the dark H in "Haa'" is actually pronounced like a "short o", and this letter's name is pronounced like Hot with the "t" bitten off: "Ho' ".

English has light and dark sounds, too, although they normally don't teach you this in school. Take a look at the light "t" in "robot". Notice how the second "o" is light, so that it should almost be spelled "robaht". It comes from the _front_ of the mouth.

Now take a look at the dark "tL" sound in "bottle". What kind of consonant is that?! It is a dark, swallowed "L" (with a "t" jammed onto the front) that comes from the back of your mouth and has a hollow, a space on the back of your tongue. In short, it's a perfect dark consonant!

Now let's check the "o" going into this. The dark L colors the sounds around it, so the "o" in "bottle" is also dark and hollow--it comes from the back of the throat.

Try it out and hear how differently the light "o" and the dark "o" are pronounced. "Robaht, bottle. Robot, bottle." So even though they are *spelled* the same, "bot", there is a big difference in how they are *pronounced* between the light "o" and the light "t" for "robot", and the dark "o" and the dark "tL" for "bottle".

And you already know how to say "bottle"!

So let's take that sound and use it to lock in the correct position for the Haa' sound, and other dark sounds. Pretend that you are an evil super-villain, like Jabba the Hutt, who is taking over the world. You laugh your hollow evil super-villain laugh -- "Bwaw--haw--haw--haw--Hawww!".

Now say "Bottle" to start this out--keep your throat in the *same position* after the L--turn the h's into Haa's, with lots of scrape in them--make sure the vowels are hollow, deep short o's, not English long O's (that would be Santa Claus!)--take a big breath, and say your new secret evil laugh out loud:
            "Bottle!  Ho'--Ho'--HHo'--HHo'-*HHHHohhhh'!*"
You should be running out of breath on the last one, so you can hear and feel the scrape in your throat.

We do this big and dramatic in practice. So then it is easy to remember the right position and do it little when you're talking in conversation.

Now you know what the hollow tongue position is like for dark letters. And you also know how to scrape your Haa's, and keep them hollow. You already knew this before--we just had to remind you that you already know this.

Remember the dark Bottle hollow tongue position for when you have to pronounce other dark letters, later on in the second book, such as Sod, Dod, Taa', and Zaa'. These all use the hollow in the back of the throat. You can already say "bottle", so these will be straightforward and simple when it comes time to learn them, as well.

# Now You Sketch It--Doodles!

# How To Write It

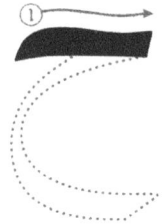

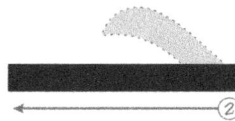

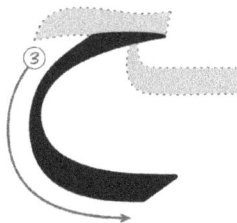

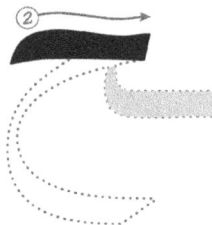

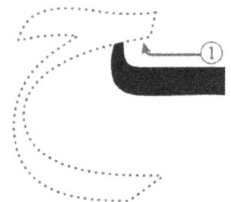

# Writing Suggestions

ح

## Stand-Alone Form
1. Start on the left, just slightly above the line. Draw a swirly stroke from left to right, to define the brim of Hot Hot Harry's Texas Hat.
2. Without lifting your pen from the paper, reverse direction and come around in a semi-circle from the top, around to the left, and down to the bottom. This defines Hot Hot Harry's open mouth. It opens way below the line. Hot Hot Harry has a big, empty mouth, so there's nothing more to write for this letter.

## Beginning Form
1. Start midway up to the left. Draw a swirling diagonal stroke from the upper left down to meet the line, or slightly above. This is the Hot Pepper Harry is Holding.
2. Without picking up the pen, reverse diraction and continue on to the next letter on the left. If you were above the line, swoop down to be on the line. That's it.

## Middle Form
1. Come in from the right from the previous letter.
2. Pick up your pen and move it to the left. Form a diagonal swooping stroke from upper left down to the right. This forms the Hot Pepper.
3. Reverse directions and continue on to the right.

## Ending Form
1. Come in from the right. End with a little rounded hook that goes straight up.
2. Pick your pen up and put it down on the left. Draw a swirling stroke that just touches the top of the hook. This is the brim of Hot Hot Harry's Hat.
3. Reverse directions and continue around in a large curve to define Hot Hot Harry's open mouth. This extends below the line. Harry's mouth is empty, so that's it.

# Writing Practice

Say the name of the letter, and make its sound,
each time you write the letter.

# Writing Practice

Now put them together.
Remember to keep each letter
separate in your mind.

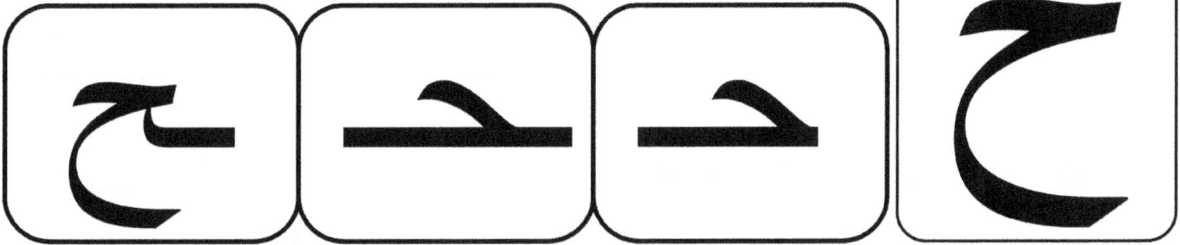

ح    ح    حـ    ـحـ    ـح

# Know The Difference!

Jeem has the gem in the middle of the measure.

جـ جـ جـ

Khaa' has the point on top.

خـ خـ خـ

Saad has a closed loop for the Sand dune, plus a little hill-crest.

صـ صـ

Daal has a duck head and a duck tail, and is open on the left.

د

ªayn looks more like a can-opener, a lamb's ribbon, or a shepherd's crook. It doesn't have the big Three Musketeer's Hot Hat on top of it.

عـ عـ عـ

Kaaf is angular, like an open "K".

كـ كـ

# Reading Practice

حار

r A H
Haarr
hot (temperature)

حب

b H
Hubb
love

جرح

H r j
jurH
hurt,
injury,
wound

حاد

d A H
Haadd
hot, spicy; sharp

حرب

b r H
Harb
war

# khaa'

**kh**

"voiceless velar fricative"

خاء

Khaa' is pronounced like a special "k" that has a lot of scrape in it, and comes from the top back of the mouth. This sound is found in English in the name of the composer Bach. It's also found in Scottish "loch", or in German "Ach".

5/7' /kh     *Khaa' CONNECTS on the left.*     kh/x/ch/ḥ

# khaa'

is Khubla Khan Bach

← *get the point*

## Khubla Khan Bach

--the khraziest
khonquering khomposer
ever to ride
the steppes of Germany!

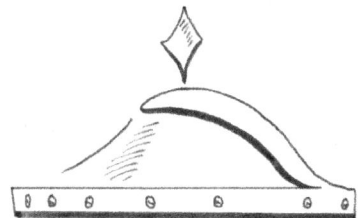

*Khan's Khap*

# Helpful Hints

Khaa' is exactly the same shape as Jeem or Haa', except with one dot above. These are the only three letters that look like this.

Like Jeem and Haa', Khaa' hangs down significantly below the line in both the ending and the stand-alone forms. It's like the loop on the bottom of a "g". You have to make sure that it goes below the line, or else it simply looks weird.

Among other differences, Haa' is pronounced with your mouth open, while Khaa' is pronounced with your mouth more closed. Haa' sounds like a scraping H, while Khaa' sounds like a scraping K that comes from the back of the throat.

# Now You Sketch It--Doodles!

# How To Write It

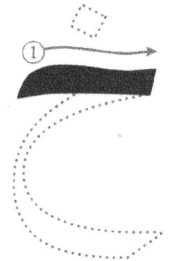

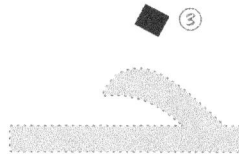

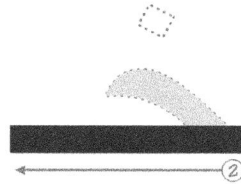

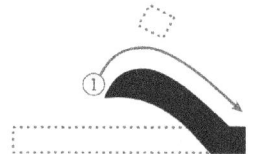

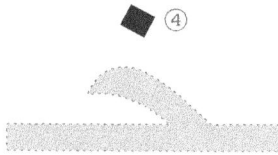

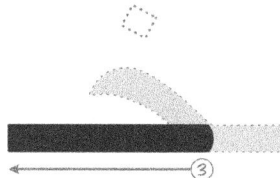

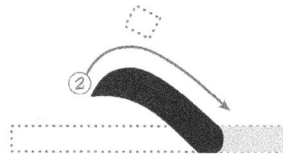

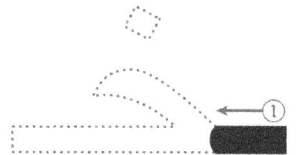

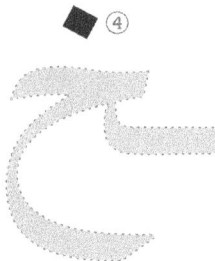

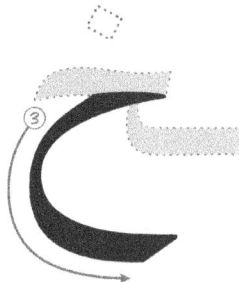

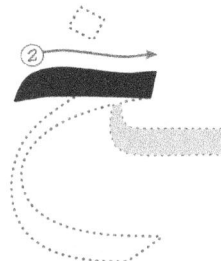

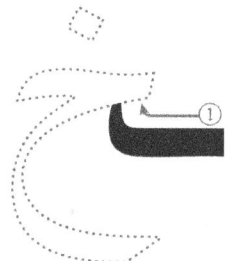

68

# Writing Suggestions

خ ځ ځ

## Stand-Alone Form
1. Start on the left. Draw a swooping stroke to the right. That's the brim of Khan's Khap.
2. Without lifting your pen, reverse directions and draw a large looping semicircle downwards. This outlines Khan's round face and his beard.
3. Now put a single dot centered on top of the figure. That's the point on top of Khan's Khap.

## Beginning Form
1. For the Beginning Form, you don't need to draw all of Khan's face--just his Khap.   Start midway up on the left side. Now draw a swooping diagonal stroke downwards to the lower right, towards the line. That's the top of his helmet.
2. Without lifting your pen, reverse direction. Continue straight on the line to the left, on to the next letter. That's the bottom of the helmet.
3. Later on, remember to come back and dot the khaa' by placing a single point on top of the first swooping stroke. That's the point on top of Khan's Khap. Remember, he wouldn't be Khubla Khan Bach if he didn't have a good point for you!

## Middle Form
1. This is similar to the Beginning Form. You're coming in from the right, from the previous letter.
2. Pick up your pen, move to the left midway up, and draw a swooping stroke to connect with the previous line. It is kind of rounded, like the top part of an old-fashioned helmet.
3. Without picking up your pen, reverse and go back to the left. Keep on going on the line, on to the next letter.
4. Later on, come back and dot the khaa'. That's the spike on top of his helmet. Remember, it's needed.

## Ending Form
1. This is similar to the Stand-Alone Form. You're coming in from the previous letter on the right. End the line with a gentle, tiny, rounded, upwards hook.
2, 3 Start on the left, and draw a swooping stroke. Reverse it to draw Khan's face as a rounded stroke.
4. Now always remember to make your point. Put the spike on his helmet, centered above. That's Khubla Khan Bach's khonquering Khap!

# Writing Practice

Say the name of the letter, and make its sound,
each time you write the letter.

# Writing Practice
Now put them together.
Remember to keep each letter
separate in your mind.

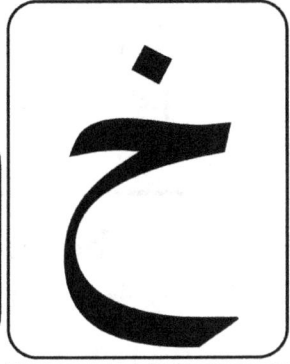

| خـ | ـخـ | ـخ | خ |
|---|---|---|---|
|  |  |  |  |
|  |  |  |  |
|  |  |  |  |
|  |  |  |  |

# Know The Difference!

Noon has one dot on top, but it is just a single nice nail, not a twisty cap.

ﻦ ﻧ ﻦ ﻦ

dhaal the souther duck mother is duck-shaped, not hat-shaped. And it does not connect on the left, it's open.

ﺫ

Zaay the zy-zy bug is more vertical-- it is shaped more like a jumping fish than a Hat. It is also open on the left.

ﺯ

Ghayn bends forwards, not backwards. It does not look like the Khap of Khan.

ﻎ

Daad is closed, not open. It has a Dune and a tiny hill-crest.

ﺽ

Fat Freddy's Faa' has a closed loop at the top.

ﻒ

# Reading Practice

خد

d kh
khadd
cheek

اخ

kh a
akh
brother

خوخ

kh w kh
khawkh
peaches

خبز

z b kh
khubz
bread

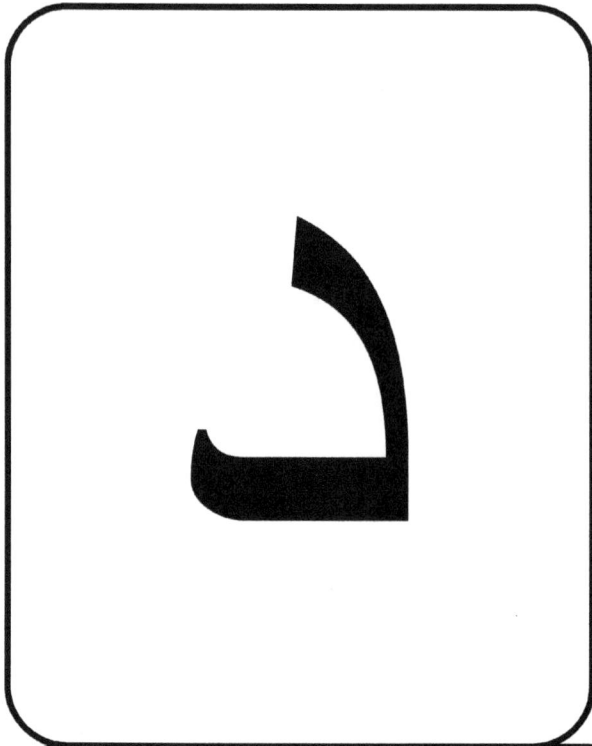

# daal

د

**d**

ح  حـ  ـحـ  ـد

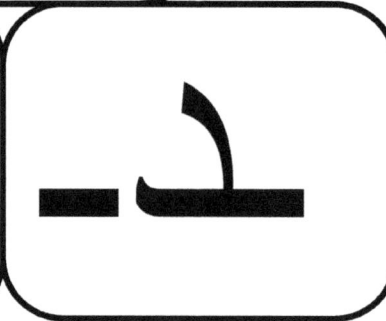

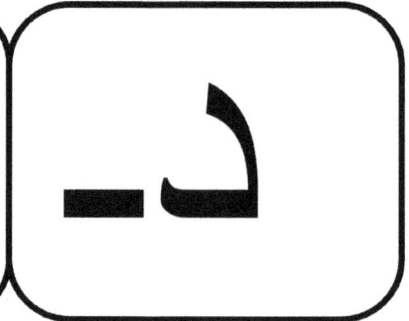

"voiced alveolar stop"

دال

daal is pronounced like a "d".
It is a light sound, coming from the front part of the
mouth just like "d" normally does.

d          *daal DOES NOT connect on the left.*          d

74

# daal

is dallas dollie's duck

delightful!
dallas dollie's daring duck
digs for dirty, damp dollars
all by itself!

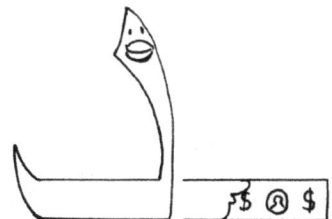

*dee-lightful dollar delivery*

# Helpful Hints

daal's name comes from the same roots as the Greek letter "delta" (Δ), which eventually became our letter "D". People got lazy in writing the right-hand corner of the delta and just turned it into a smooth curve, ᗅ, and that's how our "D" came about. And you can see that the daal is also the same letter as the delta, it's just got the left-hand side removed. You can see where maybe they *used* to draw it, because the duck-tail is there changing direction from the bottom stroke and starting to go up--the third side has just been left out in the Arabic version.

Daal is a simple letter like 'aalif that doesn't really change its shape. Also like 'aalif, it is always <u>unconnected</u> on the left-hand side.

Because it looks like a duck or a delta-triangle, daal is very different from the swooping hot pepper of Haa'.

# Now You Sketch It--Doodles!

# How To Write It

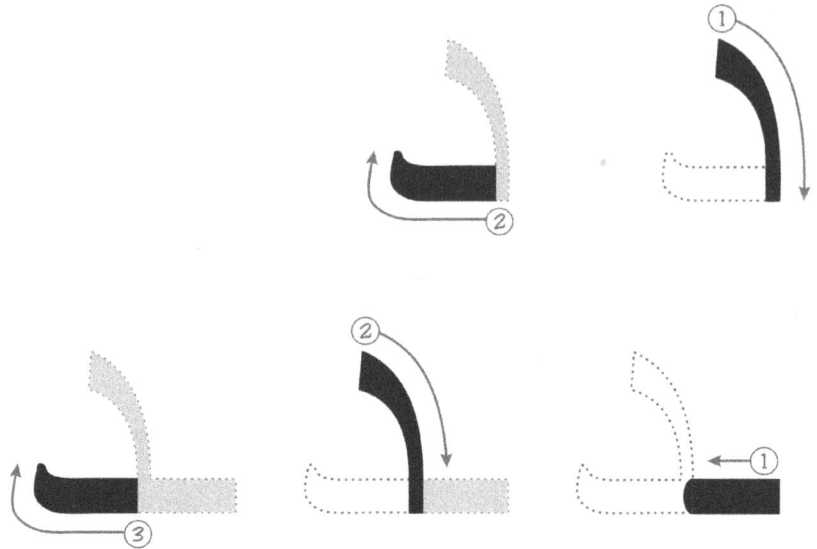

Greek delta

Arabic daal

# Writing Suggestions

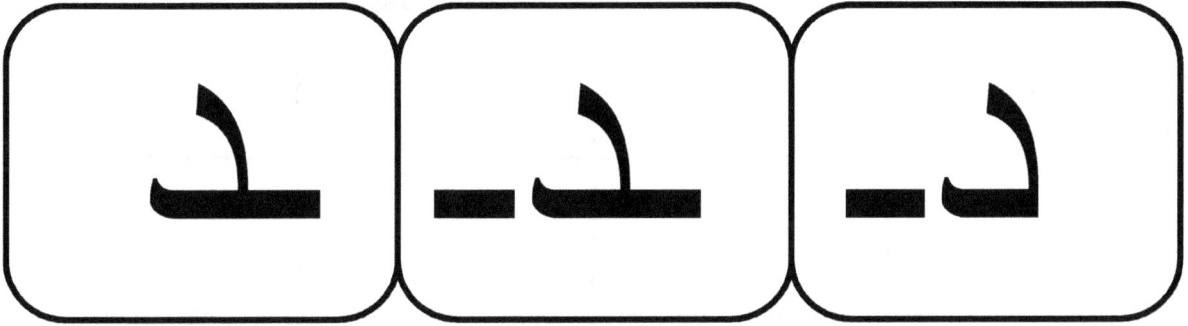

## Stand-Alone Form

1. Start in the middle, 2/3 of the way above the line. Draw a curving stroke downwards, to form the duck's head and neck. If you have a brush or a marker, start with the head thick, and then pull upwards to make the neck thin. The neck curves slightly.
2. Form the duck's body with a second stroke from right to left. Keep it straight, on the line. Hook it just a little bit by gently going upwards at the end, to make the duck's tail. Don't make the body too long or too short--it should form a "delta" triangle shape between the top of the head and the curved neck coming down. The top of the head should be over the middle of the body.

## Beginning Form

Same as the Stand-Alone Form. Leave a space after the duck tail and start the next letter with another Beginning Form, even if you're in the middle of a word.

## Middle Form

1. You're coming in from the previous letter on the right.
2. Lift the pen and put it down 2/3 of the way above the line, towards the left. Draw a curving stroke downwards to meet the line, forming the duck's head and neck. Make sure the stroke ends cleanly on the line, not above.
3. Draw a horizontal, thick, straight stroke on the line to the left, then end with a short hook. That's the duck's body and the duck's tail for the daal. Leave a space, then start the next letter with the Beginning Form, even if it's in the middle of the word.

## Ending Form

Same as the Middle Form.

# Writing Practice

Say the name of the letter, and make its sound,
each time you write the letter.

# Writing Practice

Now put them together.
Remember to keep each letter
separate in your mind.

*daal doesn't connect, but you need practice in drawing connected letters.*
*So we've put in an extra underline bar between them just for practice. Remember*
*that the following bar is not actually part of the letter--but the space gap is.*

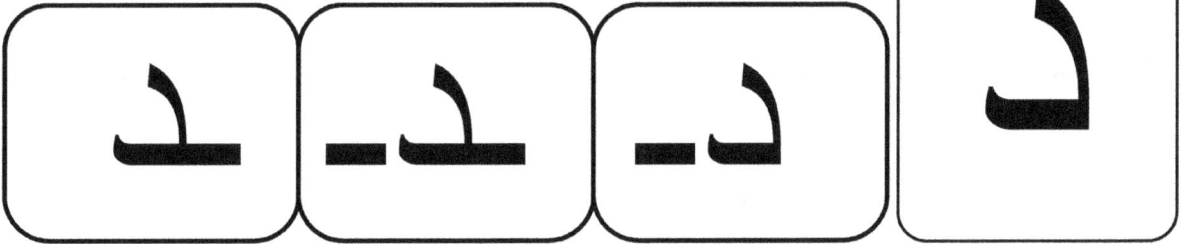

# Know The Difference!

| | |
|---|---|
| dhaal the southern duck's mother has a halo above. | ذ |
| Baa' has a dot on the Baattom. | بـ |
| Haa' is connected to the next letter on the left and looks more like a Hot Hat. | حـ |
| Kaaf is huge, it is Kris Kringle's sKi boot. It has the sKi boot bucKles inside. | كـ |
| Seen has the long wavy eyeglasses with three points on them. It is connected on the left to the next letter. | سـ |
| Roh' goes *below* the line. It is the rowing oar. It is more open, not duck-shaped. | ر |

# Reading Practice

دم

m d
damm
blood

داء

' A d
daa'
disease

جد

d j
judd
grandfather

برد

d r b
bard
cold (temperature)

جيد

d y j
jayyid
good

جديد

d y d j
jadeed
new

# dhaal

# dh

ذ    ذ    ذ

ﷲ

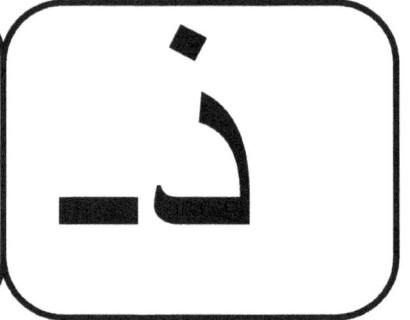

*"voiced interdental or dental fricative"*

ذال

Dhaal is supposed to be pronounced like the familiar buzzing (voiced) "th" in "that". However, in the Egyptian dialect, the tongue does not go out between the teeth and it sounds like "d" ("dat"). And the Levantine dialects, in former French colonies, have it sounding closer to "z" ("zat"). Anyway, stick with a buzzing "th", and you won't go wrong.

Dhaal is spelled "dh" to keep it separate from thaa', which is already using "th".

z/th    *Dhaal DOES NOT connect on the left.*    dh/th/dh/Dh/d

# dhaal

is the mother

*They'll remember!*
Thou blessed Southern mother
with the halo *above*,
that lathers and bathes the other
This thus shows thy love.

*Another mother...*

# Helpful Hints

Unfortunately in English the letters combination "th" stands for two different sounds--the soft "th" of "thin", and the buzzing "th" of "that". So people had to come up with a way to write the buzzing "th" sound differently in English. Using a little-known convention, someone chose "dh", and it stuck.

Probably something like "TH" might have been easier to understand, but it's too late now--everybody who's writing down Arabic using English letters is using it. It makes about as much sense as saying that "ph" sounds like "f" in "graph". Why not.

Just remember that "t" and "d" are right next to each other in sound--"t" is soft and "d" uses your voice--and so "th" and "dh" should be right next to each other in sound, too. The "th" is the soft, unvoiced one, and the "dh" is the buzzing version of th that uses your voice. We have to write down _something_ to tell them apart.

Keep the pronunciation for dhaal in the front of the mouth, up against the teeth. It's a light sound.

# Now You Sketch It--Doodles!

# How To Write It

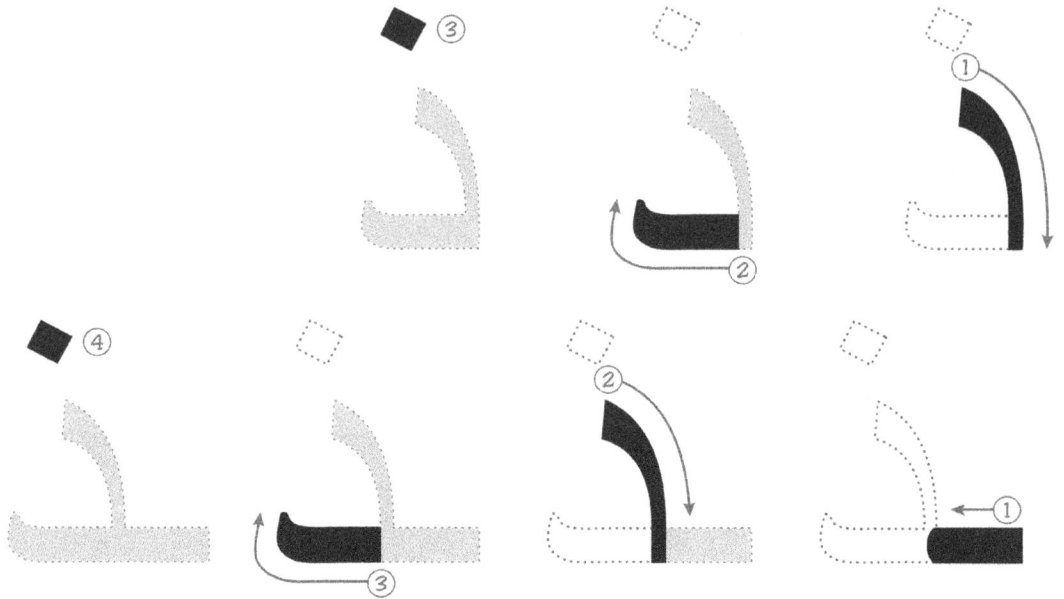

# Writing Suggestions

## Stand-Alone Form
1. Dhaal is just like daal, with an extra dot above it. Start 2/3rds of the way up, above the line, and draw a curving stroke down to the right, onto the line. This forms the mother duck's head and neck.
2. Draw a thick stroke straight along the line, twice as wide, so the top of the head sits in the middle of the stroke. That's your mother duck's body. Pull it up at the end. That's the tail.
3. Later on, come back and put a dot above the duck's head. That's the mother duck's halo. It looks like it comes out of the top of the head, which can put it anywhere from above the middle of the body to actually above the tail.

## Beginning Form
1. This is just like the stand-alone form. Start two-thirds of the way up, and draw a stroke.
2. Make a hard corner, and draw a flat line with a tail on it.
3. Later on, come back and put a dot above the figure, for the halo on the mother duck.
4. Dhaal does **not** connect on the left. So start the next letter with a Beginning form, even though it is in the middle of the word.

## Middle Form
1. You're coming in from the previous letter on the right.
2. Pick the pen up. Jump 2/3rds of the way up off the line, and 1/3 forward. Draw the neck.
3. Make a hard corner, and draw the body, with a little duck-tail at the end.
4. Come back later and put the halo above the middle of the mother.
5. Continue on and restart the next letter with a Beginning Form, even if it's inside the word.

## Ending Form
Same as the Middle Form.

# Writing Practice

Say the name of the letter, and make its sound,
each time you write the letter.

# Writing Practice

Now put them together.
Remember to keep each letter
separate in your mind.

*Remember, the following space is part of the letter...*
*but we have put in that underscore bar AFTER the space extra, so you*
*can see the space & practice connecting--it's NOT part of the letter.*

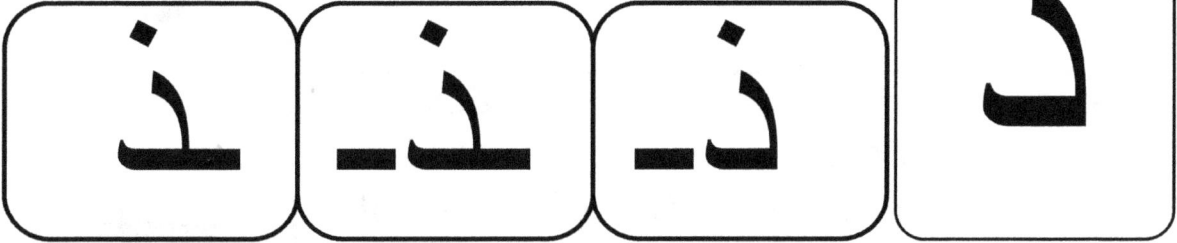

| ذ | ـذ | ـذ | ذ |
|---|---|---|---|
|   |   |   |   |
|   |   |   |   |
|   |   |   |   |
|   |   |   |   |

# Know The Difference!

daal has no halo above,
it's just an ordinary **digging duck**.

ﺩ

Noon goes more straight up and down
with its genie nails, and is **connected**
with the next letter on the left.  It is not
mother-duck shaped.

ﻨ

zaay the zy-zy bug has the jumping
fish shape and descends below the line.

ﺯ

Fat Freddy Faa' has a loop up top, and
connects to the next letter on the left.

ﻑ

Yaa' has two dots underneath,
not the other halo above.
It connects to the next letter on the left.

ﻴ

Daad is closed into a Dune shape, not
open.  It also connects to the next letter
on the left.

ﺽ

# Reading Practice

ذات

t A dh
dhaat
self

ذا

A dh
dhaa
this, this one

إذا

A dh i
idhaa
if

إذ

dh i
idh
when, as

ذاب

b A dh
dhaat
to melt, thaw

# Bonus Marks

You're doing so well, we thought we would give you a few extra symbols to learn about this week.

These symbols are not letters in the Arabic alphabet. However, they are used in words, so you should know them. They are what's called "diacritics", although some people might call them "accents". But they're not accents. In fact, they are little marks that help people remember how a word is pronounced. In Arabic, these little marks are called "Harakaat".

This week we are going to learn the three short vowels in Arabic, plus the shad-dah double consonant sign. None of these diacritics are necessary (except in the high formal writing of the Qur'aan). They are used in writings for children and foreigners. However, unless it could be confusing or there is a clear need to be unambiguous, adults will usually leave these marks out for the most part. Native speakers will get the short vowels from context, and the writing goes quicker that way.

# fat-Ha

*a*

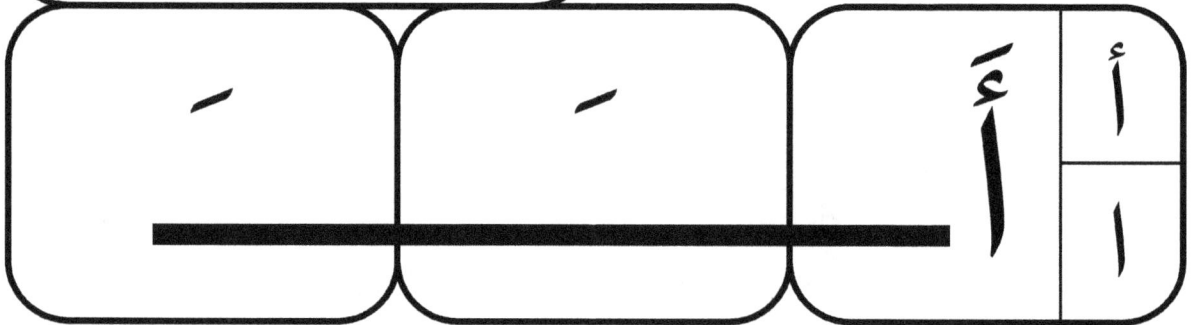

"short low back vowel"

فَتْحَة

Fat-Ha is a mark that represents the "short a". It has a **very** short duration. It is supposed to be pronounced like a fast "ah", as in "haha", or "a" as in "tradition". After a dark consonant it sounds more like a fast short "o", as in "totter". However, in some cases it is actually pronounced closer to "eh" or "uh", as in "sugar" or "about".

a/e                                                                    a

# fat-Ha

## is a big, fat Ah

Ah...

Father's one fat High eyebrow
Raised *above* his eyes
With a short Ah sound
Follows no surprise.

# Helpful Hints

There are three regular short-vowel marks in Arabic, being the fat-Ha, the kasrah, and the Dom-mah. These represent the short "a", the short "i", and the short "u" sounds, respectively.

Fat-Ha is the short "a" sound. It usually sounds like "ah" as in "father". Although it is supposed to be about the same _sound_ as 'aalif, the longer 'aalif takes twice as much time to pronounce. That's why we call the 'aalif a "long A", and write it as "aa". And we call the fat-Ha a "short a", and write it as "a". It should probably be called a "fast 'a'" and a "slow 'a'" to be different from the "short a Apple" and "long A Aim" that you learned in elementary school--but someone started a while back and unfortunately the names have stuck so far. Just remember that "short" and "long" are talking about _duration_, not the sound quality, and the rest will work itself out.

The fat-Ha's "a" sound comes **after** the consonant letter that it is above.

But think: If you want the fat-Ha to be the first letter in the word, it can't come after anything. So this is a problem. To get around this, Arabic says that you have to put in a "pretend consonant" in the writing, being a hamza riding on top of an 'Aalif, at the beginning, so the fatHa has something to come after. Because this pretend letter is only necessary for **writing**, it is not pronounced.

We will not cover the hamza until the third book, but it's that little mark that looks kind of like a small "c" on a tiny slash. Later on we'll realize that the hamza actually looks like a hamster riding a tiny surf-board. The hamza can ride on top of the 'Aalif, among other places, and the fat-Ha rides on top of the hamza.

Because the "pretend consonant" of a hamza riding an 'aalif at the beginning of a word implies that a fat-Ha _should be there_, often people don't bother to put in the fat-Ha itself in the writing. It's simply understood that the word is beginning with a fat-Ha if it has a hamza over the 'Aalif as the first letter.

Unfortunately, to make things interesting, sometimes people don't even put the hamza above the 'Aalif when they're writing fat-Ha at the beginning. They just count on context to tell the difference between a short "a" fat-Ha and a long "aa" 'Aalif. You'll have to get used to this, based on vocabulary. There's no other way to tell.

# Now You Sketch It--Doodles!

# How To Write It

# Writing Suggestions

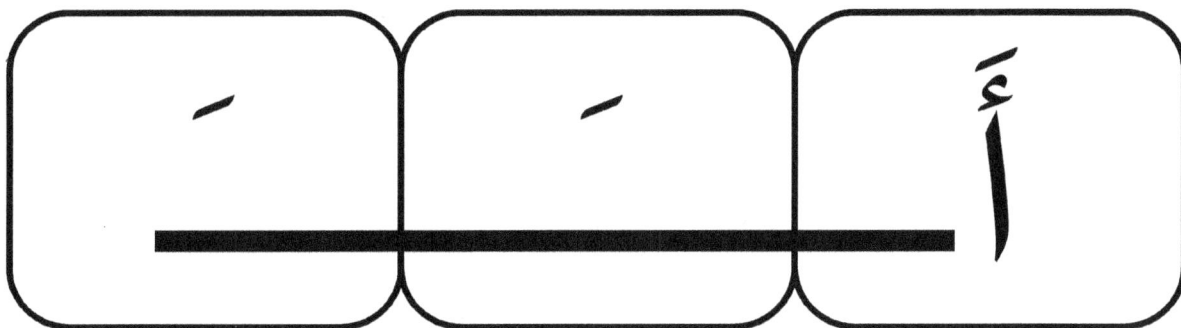

## Stand-Alone Form

1. There are only three basic short-vowel marks: fat-Ha, kasrah, and Dom-mah. Fat-Ha always floats above some other consonant letter--never by itself. So it technically has no stand-alone form. Anyway, fat-Ha is a single accent mark that starts on the upper right and slants downwards to the lower left at about 30°. Since there is no accent mark in Arabic that starts on the upper left and slants down to the lower right, the fat-Ha is both easy to recognize and easy to write.

## Beginning Form

1. We need a "pretend consonant". Draw the 'Aalif as a single, long stroke that starts a full height above the line, and goes straight down until it touches the line.
2. Now draw the hamza riding the 'Aalif. It's a tiny little "c" loop. That's the hamster.
3. Draw the tiny surfboard under the hamster at about a 30-degree angle. That's the rest of the hamza. It floats centered above the 'Aalif just like the dot above our "i"---not touching, not too high. The hamza (+ 'Aalif) forms our "pretend consonant".
4. Now you can put the fat-Ha in. Center it riding above the hamza. This is a very high stack that sticks out way tall above the line. Note that sometimes people in a hurry will leave out the fat-Ha, and sometimes even leave out the hamza.

## Middle Form

1. Same as the Stand-Alone Form. Write the fat-Ha above the middle of the other consonant letter it's riding on top of. Make it float completely above the base letter, even if it's tall. [The bar on the line here represents your base consonant.]

## Ending Form

1. Same as the Middle Form and the Stand-Alone Form.

# Writing Practice

Say the name of the letter, and make its sound,
each time you write the letter.

# Writing Practice

Now put them together.
Remember to keep each letter
separate in your mind.

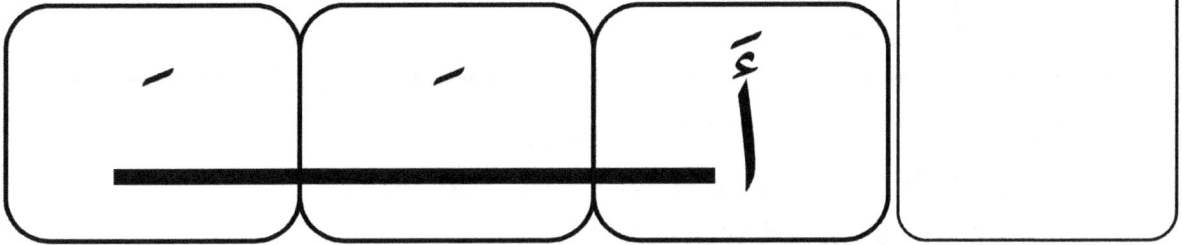

أَ

# Know The Difference!

| | |
|---|---|
| 'Aalif (A) is a real official letter, not a mark. It's longer in duration ("aa"), not rapid and brief. | ا |
| Fat-Ha-tein ("-an") is TWO slashes up on top. It has an extra N sound at the end, and only comes at the END of words. | ً |
| Kasrah ("i") and kasra-tein ("-in") are both drawn in the same right-to-left direction, but always come BELOW the line. | ِ   ٍ |
| Dom-mah ("u") has a loop at the top. It looks like a tiny blue loop of thread. Dom-matein ("-un") looks like a ruined spoon; it only comes at the end. | ُ   ٌ |
| hamza, the Uh-oh surfing hamster, has an additional tiny "c" curve up on top. It's the hamster standing on top of his surfboard. | ء |
| 'Aalif mad-dah is pronounced with a very long "'aaah". It looks like a potato-chip on top of a lift-off rocket, swirling sideways, not slanting. | آ |

# Reading Practice

أَنْتَ

a t n a
anta
you (Masc.)

أَنا

A n a
anaa
I, me

خَلّ

2 L a kh
khall
vinegar

بَنان

n A n a b
banaan
bananas

دَجاج

j A j a d
dajaaj
chicken

سَمَك

k a m a s
samak
fish

# kasrah

**i**

إ
ِ

گَسْرَة

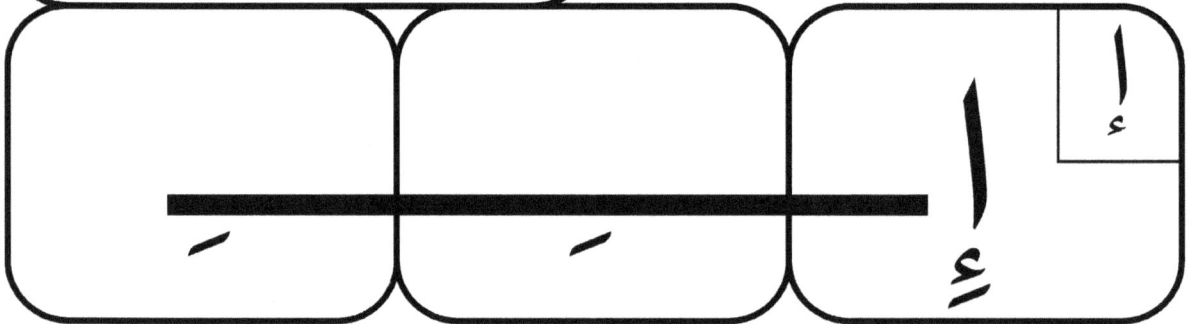

*"short high front vowel"*

Kasrah is often pronounced as a fast, short "i", as in "fish", or the "bic" in "Arabic". However, sometimes it is pronounced like "ee", only shorter, as in spanish "si" or English "Peter". And occasionally the "i" relaxes and turns into an "eh" sound, as in "bet". It is a very brief sound.

i

i, e

# kasrah

is a casserole fish

Enter in
Beneath the Sea
One casserole fish
Means short "i" or short "e"

Fishey sound
Rocking kasrah
Underground
This little fish is an itty bit of history.

# Helpful Hints

Kasrah looks just like fatHa, except it always appears **under** the line, being attached to the other letter that it is riding from underneath.

Kasrah, being a vowel, is not allowed to come at the beginning of a word by itself. Technically, it is supposed to have a consonant before it. So when a kasrah does come **at the beginning of a word**, it has to have a "pretend consonant" that it rides. The pretend consonant for kasrah is similar to that for fat-Ha, consisting of an extra 'aalif plus a hamza riding it. But in order to emphasize the "underneath" theme, the extra hamza appears on the **bottom** of the 'aalif. Then the kasrah appears under that.

Because an 'aalif with a hamza under it only appears when it is the seat for a kasrah, sometimes the kasrah is left out in printing as unnecessary. When you see a hamza underneath an 'Aalif at the beginning of a word, it **means** kasrah.

You're not supposed to leave the hamza out--when you're writing a **KASRAH** with a pretend 'Aalif and a hamza riding below, at least the hamza underneath is supposed to be **necessary**. Even when the kasrah is gone. I am sorry to say that sometimes writers do not respect this, and you just need to pick up the kasrah from context.

Of course the "pretend consonant" isn't pronounced, it's simply written.

The kasrah, being the short "i" "fish" sound, only appears under the line. Since fish only appear under water, this makes sense, and it's an easy way of remembering kasrah.

# Now You Sketch It--Doodles!

# How To Write It

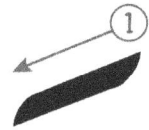

# Writing Suggestions

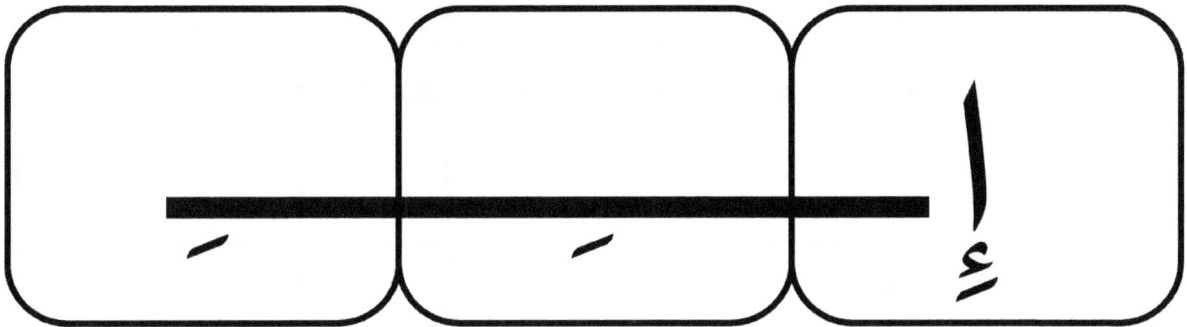

## Stand-Alone Form

1. The kasrah is drawn just like the fat-Ha, except it always comes **below** the other consonant it's riding on. Since it has to ride on top of some other letter, technically it has no stand-alone form. Anyway, the kasrah is drawn simply as a single stroke that starts at the right, and slants down to the left at about 30° (sound familiar?). It always floats **below** the line, below however deep the letter is that it's riding on.

## Beginning Form

1. Like the fat-Ha, the kasrah has to ride on some other consonant letter. But what if it actually comes at the beginning of a word? In this case, it has to ride on a "pretend consonant" that we write down, but don't actually pronounce. And in the case of the kasrah, to emphasize thinking about "below the line", we're going to write an 'Aalif with a hamza riding it on the **bottom**, and the kasra riding on the bottom of **that**. We'll learn all about the hamza later on, in Book 3. For now, just remember that, whenever you're writing a kasrah at the beginning, the little hamza always comes **below** the 'Aalif.

   So start by writing an 'Aalif. As usual, draw a full-height simple stroke straight down, from the top of where tall letters start, down to ending on the line itself.

2, 3. Draw a hamza riding **underneath** the 'Aalif. Make a small "c" shape. Keep going and make a short straight line slash, as wide as the "c", directly underneath. That's the surfboard for the hamster.

4. Now follow through with an optional kasrah slash directly under the hamza surfboard.

## Middle Form

1. The kasrah floats below the middle of whatever character it's riding on. Normally you will finish the whole word, and then come back later to put in the kasrah.

## Ending Form

Same as the Middle Form and the Stand-Alone Form.

# Writing Practice

Say the name of the letter, and make its sound,
each time you write the letter.

# Writing Practice

Now put them together.
Remember to keep each letter
separate in your mind.

ا

# Know The Difference!

| | |
|---|---|
| Fat-Ha looks exactly like kasrah, a single slash, except it always comes ABOVE the line. | َ |
| Kasra-tein is made from two kasrah slashes put together. It has an extra N, ("-in"), and only comes at the END of words. | ٍ |
| hamza looks like a tiny Uh-oh hamster on a surfboard. It can come below the line, but it has an extra "c" curve. | ء |
| baa' has a single DOT underneath, not a slanting dash. | بـ |
| Yaa' is complex. In printed form, it will always have two DOTS underneath, that's the Yippee roller skates for snakes. But in handwritten form, these are often connected together into a single dash. This dash is supposed to be flat, not tilted. But you know how it is with handwriting. Watch out for this one. | يـ<br>ىـ |
| Dom-mah, the new blue loop, looks like a tiny Wow and is pronounced "oo". It always comes ABOVE the line. | ُ |

# Reading Practice

ابن or إبن or إِبن

n b i
ibn
son

بِنت or ابنة or إبنة or إِبنة

ah n b i
ibnah
daughter

t n i b
bint
daughter

إحتِرام

m A r i t H i
iHtiraam
respect

مِشمِش

sh i m sh i m
mishmish
apricots

إسمي ...

...y m s i
ismee...
My name is ...

سِلمي

y m l i s
silmee
peaceful

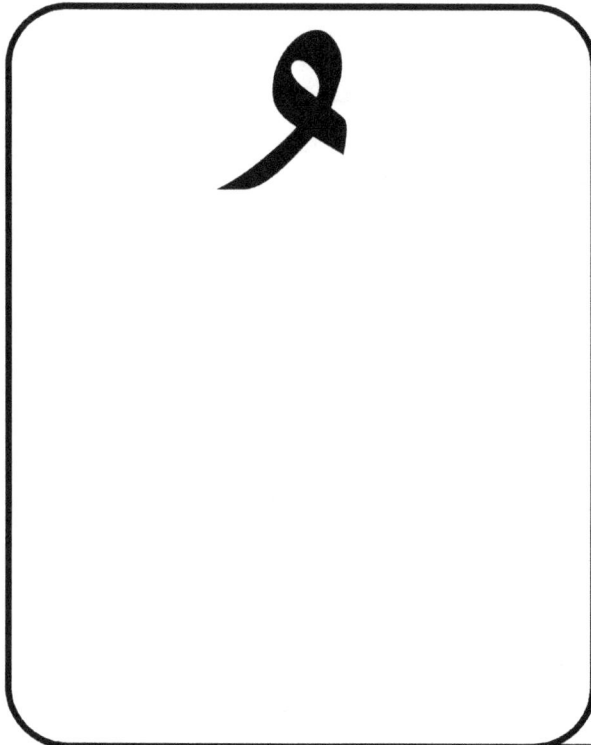

# Dom-mah

و

# u

| | | |
|---|---|---|
| و | و | أُ / أ |

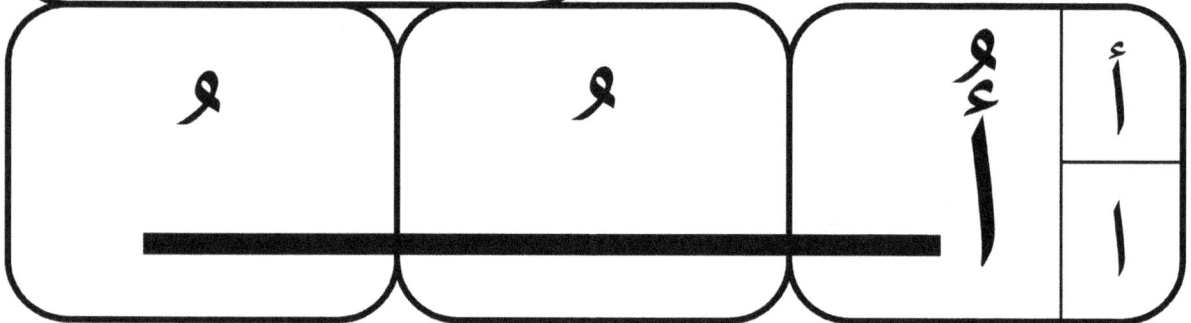

*"short high back vowel"*

ضَمَّة

Dom-mah (or spelled Damma) is typically pronounced as a brief "oo" sound, as in "To whom do you give the food?". For this reason, we write it as a single "u".

Sometimes it can also be pronounced "Oh", as in "Open".

Or it can also take a short "oo" sound as in "look".

*u/o*

u , o

# Dom-mah

## is a New Blue Loop

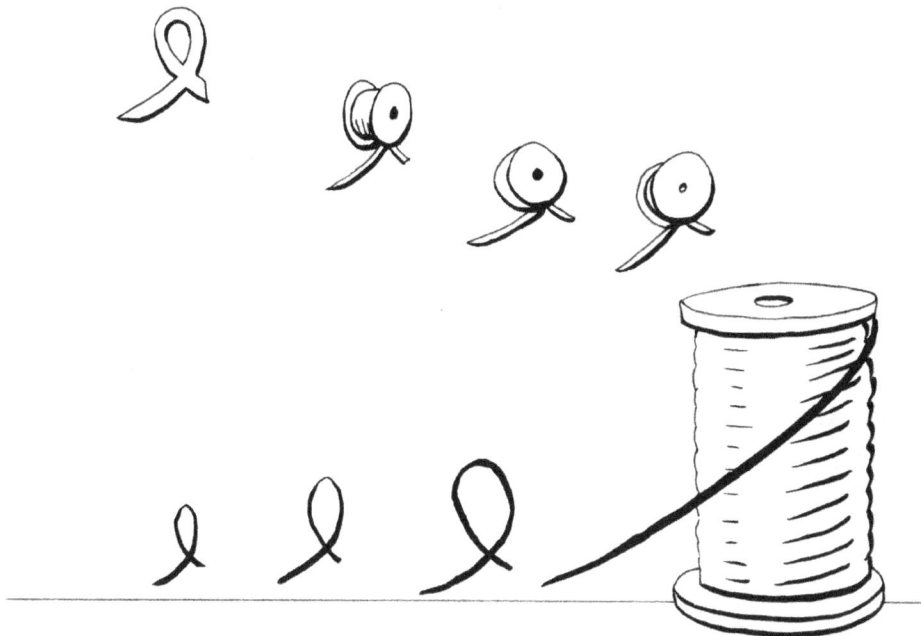

Oo look, too cool
A good new loop of blue wool
Thread from a blue spool
Soon you'll do the rule
A small comma  Called "Dom-mah"
Should make you say "oo" too!

# Helpful Hints

The Dom-mah is our third regular short vowel sound, the short "u".
The Dom-mah mark is actually a representation of the regular big "w"
letter Wow, "و", turned into a tiny accent "diacritic" mark "'".
This makes sense, because the Wow is a long uu, whereas the Dom-mah
is a short u with the same sound. We won't be learning the letter Wow
until the end of the third book, but you'll remember then.

Because the "pretend consonant" of a hamza riding an 'Aalif at the
beginning of a word implies that the Dom-mah should be there, often
people don't bother to put in the Dom-mah in the writing.
It's simply understood that the word is beginning with a Dom-mah.

By now, if you are sharp, you will have noticed that there is a problem.
Weren't we already using hamza-'aalif to stand for "fat-Ha" before?
How can you tell the difference between a hamza-'aalif that leaves the
**fat-Ha** out, and a hamza-aalif that leavss the **Dom-mah** out?

Unfortunately, the answer is "you can't, at least by the spelling alone".
You have to know what the words are, and get it from context.
And that's more advanced than we're teaching here. Sorry.

It gets more interesting. People being people, they don't want to write
anything that isn't really necessary. And that hamza sitting on top of
that 'Aalif sure is a lot of work. Both fat-Ha at the beginning, and
Dom-mah at the beginning, are allowed to be abbreviated as simply an
'Aalif all by itself. Unfortunately, sometimes people even leave out the
hamza at the bottom of a beginning kasrah. So when you see an bare
'Aalif at the **beginning** of a word all by itself, you have to be careful.
Again, you'll just have to tell the difference from context.

# Now You Sketch It--Doodles!

# How To Write It

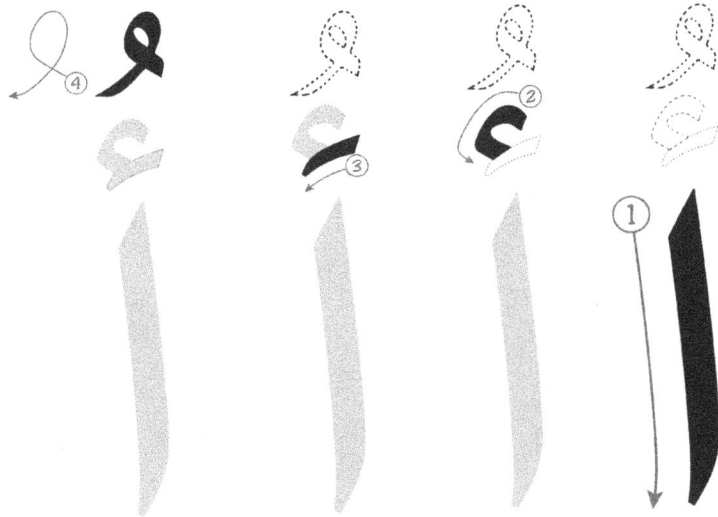

# Writing Suggestions

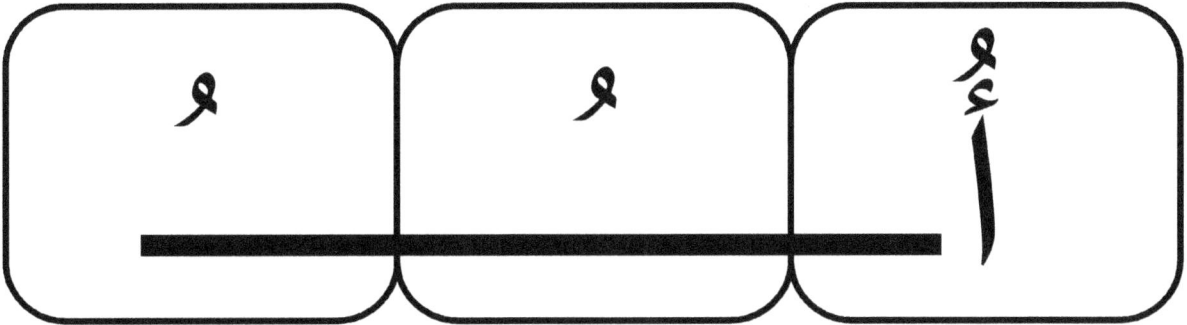

## Stand-Alone Form

1. Dom-mah is a vowel accent mark, called a "diacritic", that lets you know that the consonant letter it is over is followed by a short "u" sound. So there is no stand-alone form, unless you're simply talking about the mark itself. The Dom-mah is always based on top of some other letter, some consonant. Anyway, a Dom-mah is drawn in a single, looping stroke. Start on the right side, go up, around, and sweep down to the left. Although the loop looks a little like a tiny "9" on its side, make sure to cross just a bit in front of where you start, so there's a teeny loose end hanging out on the right. The Dom-mah hangs downwards at around 45° or 50°, usually slightly more than the ordinary 30° slant given to a fat-Ha, a kasrah, or the surfboard of a hamza.

## Beginning Form

1. A Dom-mah is not supposed to start a word by itself, since it rides on top of some other letter. In the rare cases that it **does** start the word, you have to give it an extra hamza plus an 'aalif to ride on. These are not pronounced. You'll learn about hamza later on in Book 3, so don't worry about it for now. ...To start, write an 'Aalif normal-size by starting at the full height above the line, and drawing a single stand-alone stroke straight down to the line. The hamza, plus the required 'Aalif under it, will make up the "pretend consonant".
2. Draw the hamza above the 'Aalif. Make a small "c" loop that goes around. It floats on top of the 'Aalif like the dot on a letter "i"--not too high, not low.
3. Finish the hamza with a straight stroke, kind of similar to the crosspiece on a capital "G", except underneath. This slants down at about 30°. The back end of the surfboard lines up with the left side of the hamster. The front end sticks out slightly.
4. Now draw a Dom-mah loop centered above the hamza. It's optional but recommended. The big end hangs down at around 45°. The entire stack is way taller than the normal letters.

## Middle Form

1. Same as the Stand-Alone Form. Draw the Dom-mah above the middle of the other consonant letter it's riding on.

## Ending Form

1. Same as the Middle and Stand-Alone Forms.

# Writing Practice

Say the name of the letter, and make its sound,
each time you write the letter.

# Writing Practice

Now put them together.
Remember to keep each letter
separate in your mind.

| ه | ه | أُ | ه |
|---|---|---|---|
| | | | |
| | | | |
| | | | |
| | | | |

# Know The Difference!

Fat-Ha has no loop. It sounds like "ah".
The dash slants more sideways, not down.

ﹷ

Dom-matein, the ruined spoon of Brigadoon,
is almost like two Dom-mahs put together.
It is pronounced with an extra N at the end, "oon",
and only comes at the end of words.

ﹲ

Sukuun has a loop, but no tail.

ﹿ

Wow is a full letter, not a tiny vowel helper mark.
It is much larger. It comes in-line with the other
letters in the word, not riding above. And it
stretches below the line.

و

fat-Ha-tein is two slashes that are disconnected.
It only comes at the end of a word.

ﹰ

The buckle in the ski boot in Ending Kaaf is not a
vowel-mark at all, it's part of the letter.

ﻚ

# Reading Practice

هُم

m u h
hum
they

هُوَ

a w u h
huwa
he

جُبن

n b u j
jubn
cheese

خُبز

z b u kh
khubz
bread

أُعيدُ

u d y ª u
uªeedo
I report

حُمُّص

S u2m u H
Hum-muS
hummus

125

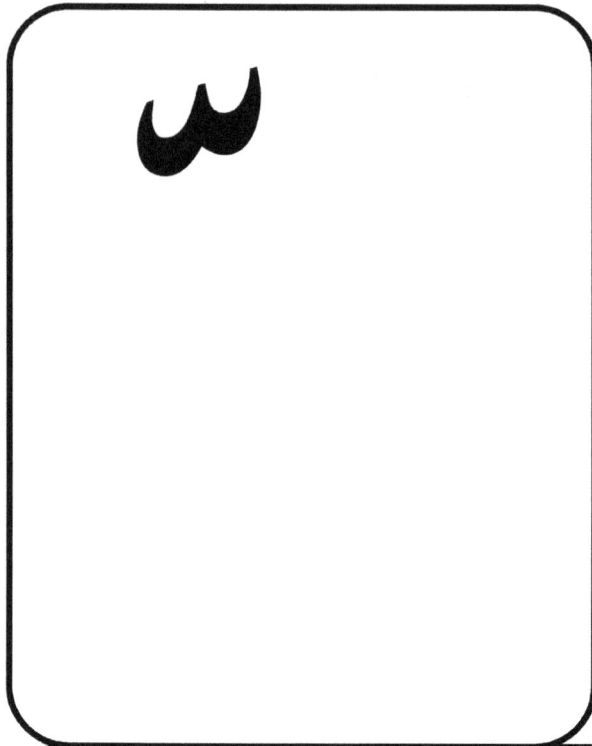

# shad-dah

(repeat and double the length of the previous consonant)

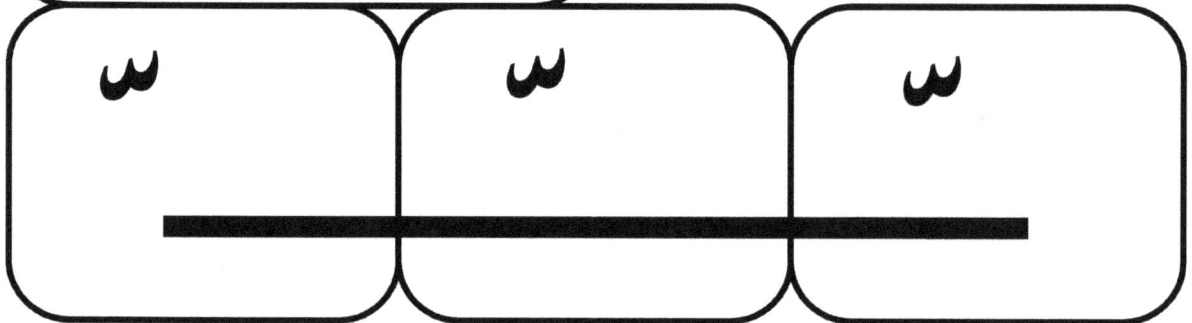

شَدَّة

*"gemination"*

Shad-dah is a special sign that tells you to <u>double</u> the consonant that it is over. So you pronounce that consonant twice, or twice as long. Think of the difference in the "d" sounds between "trader" and "mid-day". Or the difference in the "n" sounds between "unit" and "unnecessary". In English letters, we will write the consonant that the shad-dah is over **twice**, sometimes putting a dash in the middle.

# shad-dah

is the double-u bongo drums in the sky

Double-U up in the sky
shad-dah-shad-dah bongo drums

Hit it, hit it twice-twice
Sounds so, sounds so nice-nice

Double-double consonants
shad-dah sounds
Two sounds!
Better than one!

# Helpful Hints

Shad-dah looks like a little double bongo-drum set. This can be flat, but it's normally tilted slightly, at about 30°, with the horns up.

It reminds you to hit the sound twice.

Shad-dah asks you to finish the one sound completely, then start it up again. So you really do say the consonant twice, it's not just one sound that is twice as long.* So it's much better to spell it with a dash in the middle. And then pronounce it just the way it's spelled. Yes, it does make a difference.

It always floats up ABOVE the letter it's riding.

Shad-dah only goes over _consonants_. So if you ever see a shad-dah together with a short vowel mark such as a fat-Ha, a kasrah, or a Dom-mah, you'll know to double the _consonant_ that the shad-dah is over, and then add the short vowel _afterwards_.

In the case that a short vowel such as a fat-Ha or a Dom-mah is on the same letter as a shad-dah, the shad-dah comes **first**, because it modifies the _consonant_, and then the fat-Ha or Dom-mah vowel rides above, floating directly on _top_ of the shad-dah. Because the short vowel comes _next, after_ the consonant. This can make the stack pretty tall sometimes. See the Reading Practice section for some examples.

You don't need to worry about a shad-dah colliding with a kasrah, because the shad-dah is _always_ on the _top_, above the consonant, whereas the kasrah is _always_ below the line.

Unfortunately, some people leave the shad-dah out when they are in a hurry. This is not good form, but people are allowed to do it anyway. Please always put your own shad-dahs in; but be aware that sometimes others will leave them out.

* Naturally, this is similar to the "chiisai tsu" sign in Japanese. But you knew that already.

# Now You Sketch It--Doodles!

# How To Write It

# Writing Suggestions

ﺵ          ﺵ          ﺵ

## Stand-Alone Form

Like most of the marks, it does not make sense to talk about the Stand-Alone form of this sign, because it's not a real letter. But here's how you draw it:

1. Start on the right side. We're going to draw two tiny u's right next to each other. The horns are pointing straight up. But the tops of the horns, and the bottoms of the u's, are usually on an invisible line slanted downwards at about 30°. So they are parallel to the same slant that a fat-Ha makes.

So draw a tiny rounded u, from right to left--but when you're coming up on the second horn, stop a little bit early--it's a little bit lower than the first horn.

2. Without picking up your pen, draw another tiny u in the same fashion. Down, then up, right to left. The tips of the three horns on top should all line up together on a straight line slanted down slightly. And the tips of the rounded bottoms of the u's should also line up, on a line with the same slope. This might take a little practice.

## Beginning Form

It doesn't make any sense for a word to start with a shad-dah itself, since the shad-dah changes a separate consonant letter that's already there. And normal words don't start with a doubled consonant, unless you count the change in sound from "sun" letters combining with "al". But if you had to follow an Ending Form, the Beginning Form is simply made by labeling the consonant you want to mark. You do this by simply putting a shad-dah above it, sometimes slightly to the left.

## Middle Form

Draw the shad-dah above or slightly on the left side of the letter you are modifying.

## Ending Form

It might seem surprising that you can have a doubled consonant at the end, but this is a relatively popular combination. Draw it the same as the others.

131

# Writing Practice

Say the name of the letter, and make its sound,
each time you write the letter.

# Writing Practice

Now put them together.
Remember to keep each letter
separate in your mind.

*As usual, the bar here is just a stand-in for the other letter
you're going to be drawing the shad-dah mark over.*

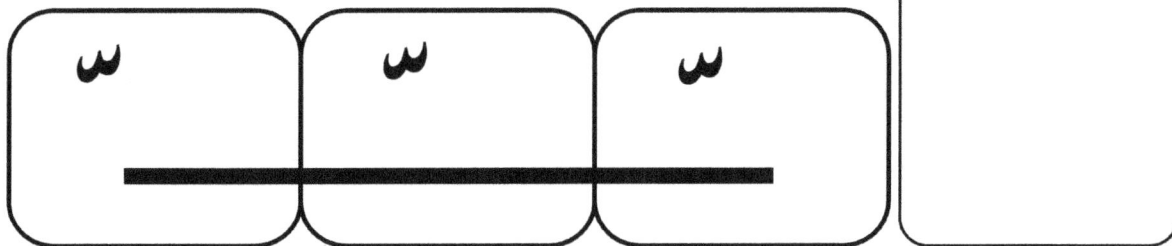

ﺵ

ﺵ   ﺵ   ﺵ

# Know The Difference!

| | |
|---|---|
| seen also looks like a "w", but it is large. It sits directly on the line as part of the other letters. In contrast, shad-dah always is small and floats *above* some other letter. | سـ |
| Fat-Ha also floats above, but it's a straight line, not curves. | ́ |
| Dom-matein looks more like a ruined spoon. It has a complete loop up top, and the bent spoon handle bends outwards, not up. It used to be two spoons together, but they got lazy drawing the rest of the second one. | ٞ |
| Sukuun is only a single circle. | ه |
| The three dots above sheen or thaa' are actually part of the letter, not an extra mark. They can turn into a connected upside-down "v" in handwriting. | شـ ثـ |
| Fat-Ha-tein is two slashes, not two "u"'s. And it only comes at the end of words. | ً |

# Reading Practice

أرزّ

2z r a
aruzz
rice

حَيّ

2y aH
Hayy
live (adj.)

جِدّاً

an 2d i j
jid-dan
very

أَيُّ

u2y a
ay-yu
which

تُفّاح

H A 2f u t
tuf-faaH
apples

اللَّيل

L y a2L L a
al-laeel
the night

الثُّلُث

th u L u2th L a
ath-thuluth
the third (time)

خَلاّب

b 2LA a kh
khal-laab
pretty (place, thing)

# Congratulations!

You have faithfully completed all of the exercises in the book. You are now a new person!

"The mind, once expanded to the dimensions
of larger ideas, never returns to its original size."
Oliver Wendell Holmes

To certify your accomplishment, we are here including a "Certificate of Completion" for you.

If you have an instructor, or if there is someone else who is teaching the course for you, you can have them sign your certificate for you.

If you're teaching the course to yourself, sign the certificate yourself after you've completed all the exercises and you know you deserve it.

Why not carefully tear your certificate out of the book, and post it on the wall where you can see it. It will remind you to be proud of your accomplishments. This will help focus your mind, so that you will become even stronger and more successful. Go for it!!

# Certificate of Completion

## This is to certify that

_____

has successfully completed

### Week 1

### Actually Learn Arabic Letters

and is fully entitled to receive all the benefits thereof

from this day onward

all through life.

Awarded this day

_____
date of achievement

_____
Signatory Authority

"The bold fonts make the letters easy to read. And the creative illustrations make the letters easy to remember. It's a fun and easy way for anyone to learn the Arabic alphabet."

Wendy Radwan, UCLA student


"I can't believe how interesting this is! It's not boring at all! The way the pictures stick in your mind, somehow it made me just want to keep reading it. And I found myself recognizing letters in the reading practice after only a few seconds of looking at the pictures. I couldn't believe it. This is the best course in learning Arabic letters I've ever seen. Anyone who needs to learn Arabic definitely needs to get this course."

Cora Mamerto, housewife


Go ahead and check out
http://www.authoritybooks.com/arabic.html
for some free stuff that will help you out.


AUTHORITY BOOKS, INC.  AUSTIN, TX

www.ingramcontent.com/pod-product-compliance
Lightning Source LLC
Chambersburg PA
CBHW081329090426
42737CB00017B/3064